PASTORAL COUNSELING & COACHING

Compass Therapy in Churches

By

Dan Montgomery, Ph.D.

Note: This book does not take the place of professional counseling or supervision. Case studies are composites that de-identify counselees or offer hypothetical scenarios.

To order: www.CompassTherapy.com

Compass Therapy® and Self Compass® are registered trademarks of Dan & Kate Montgomery.

Editing: Kate Montgomery. Cover Design: David Gagne. Photo credit: David O'Dell.

Compass Works
1482 East Valley Rd, Ste 301
Montecito, CA 93108

All Scripture quotations, unless otherwise indicated, are taken from the HOLY BIBLE, NEW INTERNATIONAL VERSION®. NIV®. Copyright © 1973, 1978, 1984 by International Bible Society. Used by permission of Zondervan. All rights reserved.

ISBN: 978-0-557-19487-2
Printed in the United States of America

Library of Congress Cataloguing-in-Publication Data
Montgomery, Dr. Dan
Pastoral Counseling and Coaching/Dr. Dan Montgomery
p.   cm.
ISBN 978-0-557-19487-2
1. Pastoral counseling. 3. Pastoral Care. 3. Pastoral Psychotherapy. 2. Pastoral Ministry. 5. Christian Counseling. 5. Biblical Counseling. 7. Chaplaincy. 8. Compass Therapy. 9. Self Compass.

ABOUT THE AUTHOR

Dr. Dan Montgomery has held dual licensure as a Psychologist and Marriage & Family Therapist for thirty years. He has served as a professor of counseling and psychotherapy at Pepperdine University Graduate School of Psychology and the University of New Mexico.

Dr. Montgomery has trained and supervised pastoral counselors in graduate schools, churches, counseling centers, and the chaplaincy. His Compass Therapy model applied in this book is praised by professors at Yale Divinity School, University of Notre Dame, Princeton Theological Seminary, Stanford University School of Medicine, Fuller Seminary, Gordon-Conwell Seminary, Oral Roberts University, Santa Clara University, Southwestern Baptist Seminary, Garrett-Evangelical Seminary, Westmont College, Assemblies of God Theological Seminary, Bangor Theological Seminary, Denver Seminary, Andover Newton Theological School, Pentecostal Theological Seminary, Midwestern Baptist Seminary, Dallas Theological Seminary, Southwestern Assemblies of God University, Lee University, and Loyola University Chicago— and by Cardinals in six countries, including the Vatican.

As a professor of psychology and counseling, Dan has taught graduate and undergraduate courses in general psychology, physiological psychology, theories of personality, theories of counseling, psychological testing, group dynamics, psychodrama, clinical psychology, advanced techniques of counseling and psychotherapy, human sexuality, advanced psychopathology, group counseling and therapy, psychology of religion, psychology of women, counseling supervision and practicum, and clinical internship.

Dan Montgomery is dedicated to making the principles of Compass Therapy available to pastors, counselees, and churches throughout the world. His books that intersect pastoral counseling include:

COMPASS PSYCHOTHEOLOGY:
Where Psychology & Theology Really Meet

CHRISTIAN COUNSELING THAT REALLY WORKS:
Compass Therapy In Action

CHRISTIAN PERSONALITY THEORY:
A Self Compass for Humanity

THE SELF COMPASS:
Charting Your Personality in Christ

COMPASS THERAPY:
Christian Psychology in Action

Dr. Montgomery's online course, *Pastoral Counseling: The Intersection of Psychology and Spirituality*, offers 4 CE Credits for psychologists, MFTs & LCSWs (BBS), Social Workers (ASWB), Nurses (BRN), and Counselors (NBCC, NAADAC). Preview or order at www.ZurInstitute.com.

COMMENDATIONS FOR *PASTORAL COUNSELING & COACHING: COMPASS THERAPY IN CHURCHES*

YALE DIVINITY SCHOOL

"Veteran pastoral counselor Dan Montgomery has given us a breezy, fast-reading manual that takes the mystery out of the helping work of the action-oriented counselor. His wisdom opens windows with helpful metaphors and lively case studies."
—*Gaylord Noyce, Professor Emeritus of Pastoral Theology*

ORAL ROBERTS UNIVERSITY

"It is not easy to find a personality theory that correlates well with sound biblical anthropology. Dan Montgomery's Compass Therapy provides a synthesis that allows biblically sound and theologically balanced pastoral counseling practice that does not betray the essentials of Trinitarian theology or psychological theory.

The Compass Model is comprehensive, Christ-conscious, pragmatic and pastoral. There is room in this model for professional perception, pastoral prayer and the power of the Paraclete. It provides a whole person frame of reference to assess persons trapped in unhealthy patterns of life and to guide them on a journey toward wholeness. This is a growth-oriented healing model that can take place in congregations as well as counseling centers."
— *Thomson K. Mathew, Ph.D., Professor of Pastoral Care & Dean, School of Theology and Missions*

PRINCETON THEOLOGICAL SEMINARY

"The Compass Therapy Model for pastoral counseling makes a very important statement about how the Christian faith and psychology can work together to bring God's healing into congregational life. The case studies are excellent. Montgomery uses a wide range of techniques including role-play and imaging, which are helpful and empowering to persons."
— *Abigail Rian Evans, Ph.D., Charlotte Newcombe Professor of Practical Theology Emerita; Author, "Negotiated Death: Is God Still At the Bedside?"*

FULLER THEOLOGICAL SEMINARY

"The Compass Therapy approach to pastoral counseling delivers the Human Nature Compass, a growth tool that helps pastors discern what's going on in a counselee's mind and heart, body and spirit. This increases pastoral competence in understanding counselees and meeting their needs.

Dan Montgomery's well-established Compass Model integrates psychology and theology in a highly effective way. I commend this book as a superb resource to all who serve their church and community in pastoral care and counseling."
— *Ray S. Anderson, Ph.D., Senior Professor of Theology and Ministry*

MIDWESTERN BAPTIST THEOLOGICAL SEMINARY

"As a teacher preparing pastors and counselors to provide care, I include the Compass Model as a significant part of the courses I teach. Compass Therapy provides a simple and efficient model to use that is clinically sound and applies Christian principles as the source for healing. It equips both pastors and therapists to provide effective care."
— *Larry Cornine, Ph.D., Professor of Pastoral Counseling*

ASSEMBLIES OF GOD THEOLOGICAL SEMINARY

"The church of the 21st century desperately needs pastors and pastoral counselors who are psychologically educated and spiritually discerning to address the complex emotional and psychological needs of today's congregants.

This book provides a biblically-based and psychologically sound perspective on human growth and behavior, as well practical techniques for effective therapeutic intervention. It will definitely help pastors and pastoral counselors find more satisfaction and success in pastoral counseling.

I commend Dr. Montgomery for his contribution to the field of pastoral counseling and highly recommend his Compass Therapy Model as a framework for pastoral care."
— *Rev. Melody D. Palm, Psy.D., Associate Professor, Director of Psychology and Counseling Program*

DALLAS THEOLOGICAL SEMINARY

"Through the Compass Model framework and the many techniques Dan Montgomery utilizes, you see examples of Christ's love coming alive in the pastoral counseling session. I appreciate his many insights and focus on healing the whole person—body, mind, emotions and spirit. This is what good Christian counseling looks like!"
— *Linda Marten, Ph.D., Department of Biblical Counseling*

GORDON-CONWELL THEOLOGICAL SEMINARY

"An exceptionally practical book for pastors who need to find effective ways to help those in the congregation who are struggling with a variety of issues. As usual, with books in the 'Compass' series, the work is consistent with biblical truth as the foundation for pastoral intervention. A useful addition to the working library of pastor and seminarian."
— *Raymond F. Pendleton, Ph.D., Professor of Pastoral Care*

BANGOR THEOLOGICAL SEMINARY

"This book is full of practical wisdom for students, pastors and pastoral counselors. Through years of his own effective pastoral practice and teaching, it is clear that Dan Montgomery understands the beautiful potential of healing energy available in the pastor and care-seeker relationship. Dr. Montgomery integrates the approaches of so many esteemed counselors—from Carl Jung to Carl Rogers—along with many more contemporary theorists, in forming his own well-proven Compass Therapy approach.

I am impressed with how the author takes complex material from the worlds of clinical diagnostics and personality disorder theory, blends it with his own pastoral counseling experiences, and brings it to the reader as the Compass Model for pastoral work, an approach that is both easily understood and very helpful."
— *Ron Baard, Ph.D., Professor of Pastoral Studies*

LOYOLA UNIVERSITY CHICAGO

"Dan Montgomery encourages pastoral workers to reclaim the Church as a 'natural home' for human growth and development. The Compass Model offers clear and concrete suggestions for assisting persons to move toward healthier functioning and Christ-centered living."
— *Diane Maloney, D.Min., LCPC, Clinical Assistant Professor of Pastoral Counseling*

SOUTHWESTERN ASSEMBLY OF GOD UNIVERSITY

"*Pastoral Counseling & Coaching* is a comprehensive approach to Pastoral Counseling. Montgomery's text is a priceless resource for students, pastors, and professionals in the field."
— *Jeff Logue, Ph.D., Licensed Professional Counselor*

CONTENTS

PART I:
INTRODUCTION TO PASTORAL COUNSELING AND COACHING

1. Pastoral Counseling & Coaching Overview

The Compass Therapy approach to pastoral counseling and coaching brings simple yet sophisticated tools into the pastoral ministry domain. The compass model fluidly integrates polarities like the relationship between Christ's personality and human personality, the rhythm between Scripture and psychology in pastoral care, and an understanding of rigidity versus actualizing growth in a counselee's life.

As you will see, the compass model helps you discern the cognitive, emotional, physiological, and spiritual dimensions of a counselee's life (*Human Nature Compass*), yielding several avenues for intervention at any given moment.

In applying the compass model you will learn how to perceive crucial elements of a counselee's personality and relationships within a first session (*The Self Compass*). This honing of your counseling intuition will make your pastoral counseling active and effective, leading to greater success and satisfaction for both you and your counselees.

Other applications of the compass model, such as Christ's Self Compass, make God's personality intelligible to people. When drawing upon the insights this model offers, people begin to understand that they really are created in the image of God for love and friendship with the Father, Son, and Holy Spirit. Not only this, but they begin to bond with one another more deeply, a sure mark of a healthy church.

Compass Therapy infuses a biblically grounded Christian orthodoxy with empirically validated research in personality and counseling, offering an overall counseling method ideally suited for pastoral care within churches and people-helping ministries. In this book I use the term "counselee" to designate the recipient of pastoral counseling. The term is interchangeable with "client" or "parishioner" if that is your preference.

In defining the scope of this book, I have deliberately paired pastoral counseling with coaching to underscore what many pastors have told me they need: a practical method for interacting with parishioners that promotes people's understanding of self and God, reconciliation with others, ability to cope with the crises faced throughout the lifespan, and motivation to integrate their Christian faith with the challenges of daily life.

The *counseling* aspect of this book presents a Christian personality theory and method for pastoral counseling intervention that sizes up factors disrupting a person's life and offers growth strategies that move a person forward toward resolution.

The *coaching* aspect responds to a counselee's need to feel emotionally significant and understood by a caregiver, especially during times of vulnerability. When you exercise the coaching function of pastoral counseling, you build people up by providing an occasional pep talk, praying with them for God to show his loving guidance, or offering an encouraging word when they feel dispirited.

In counseling you listen with the third ear (a form of hearing that requires discernment in psychological and spiritual causes and effects), whereas in coaching you impart enthusiasm and faith that strengthens motivation. Both are needed in pastoral ministry, since a pastoral counselor functions more as a consecrated shepherd of Christ than as a state licensed therapist.

By the time you finish this book, you will have put together pastoral counseling and coaching in a way that brings you fulfillment and serves your constituency well.

Why Compass Therapy?

The use of Compass Therapy in churches equips a new generation of pastoral counselors with practical tools that bring together spiritual faith, psychological insight, a Christian personality theory, and the use of counseling techniques to engage and heal the brokenness in a counselee's personality and human nature.

But why, you may ask, use the word therapy at all? Doesn't therapy imply a secular approach to counseling carried out by mental health professionals? The answer is that major contributions to pastoral counseling have arisen from psychoanalysis, Jungian therapy, Transactional Analysis, Gestalt therapy, Client-centered therapy, and Cognitive-behavioral therapy. What distinguishes them is generally a tradition of empirical research and clinical validity. However, these methodologies stand outside the Christian tradition, and some of their assumptions flatly contradict orthodox Christian teachings. While elements of these approaches have been adapted for church use, it is often because no Christian equivalent exists. Pastors and parishioners have rightly complained from time to time that these secular psychologies have undermined their trust in the Bible, the Trinity, and the Church.

In contradistinction, Compass Therapy has its origins in both scientific research and biblical Trinitarian theology. While hundreds of studies validate the growth psychology behind compass theory, the core assumption is that Jesus of Nazareth reveals God's personality and interpersonal nature, a nature known as the Trinity, and becomes the standard against which personality health and dysfunction are discerned. While it might seem to some that Jesus' personality would have nothing to do with modern conceptions of personality, compass theory proposes the opposite: that Christ's personality and behavior are readily understood through the contemporary lens of the Self Compass growth tool, the central working model of Compass Therapy that points the way to mental health while illuminating the personality disorders described in the *Diagnostic and Statistical Manual of Mental Disorders (DSM).*

I deal with this application as it pertains to pastoral counseling and coaching in Part Three: The Self Compass. But for now I want to underscore that Compass Therapy signifies a counseling approach backed by empirical research and differentiated from other counseling theories by a Christian ontological foundation.

Whether you are a pastor, seminary student, or church-affiliated therapist, I view you as a companion in the field of pastoral counseling. I will present theoretical and practical principles with this in mind. Together we share a joint commission from Christ to love and to heal. We seek to help people develop greater wholeness, liberating them from constraints that block fulfillment, strengthening their participation in knowing themselves and doing God's will.

My own calling as a psychologist and pastoral counselor has extended over thirty years. During that time I have persistently encouraged pastors, chaplains, and Christian therapists to take back the high ground of counseling, an opportunity for ministry that in the twentieth century was too often relinquished to mental health professionals.

Christ In Pastoral Counseling

While the world benefits from psychiatrists, psychotherapists, and marriage and family counselors, no one can take the place of Christ's pastoral shepherds, appointed by the Lord and empowered by the Holy Spirit, spending countless hours calming the anxious, encouraging the depressed, binding up the emotionally wounded: Maria, Bill, Antonio,

Ming, Abdul. Through his pastoral ministers, Christ reaches out in every culture not only to save people from sin and set them right with God, but to help them grow psychologically and spiritually, creating in them a sound mind and responsive heart, a relaxed body and serene spirit, edifying them with enough maturity to love others as they learn to love themselves and God.

During my seminary years, a classmate of mine I will call Jeff developed suicidal urges; his study of the Bible had left him with the impression that he had too many sins for God to forgive. Though there was a professional counselor on staff, this student chose to confide his soul-pain to a professor of Old Testament, himself an ordained minister. What struck me was how the professor took time out of his schedule to shepherd and nurture Jeff, even to the point of visiting him in the dorm at night to make sure he was okay. After several days of being watched over, Jeff's depression lifted. He told me that the professor's faithful caring had penetrated his emptiness, opening an inner door through which he experienced God's love.

Christianity Needs Psychologically Informed, Spiritually Attuned Pastoral Counselors

Churches offer a natural home for personal development throughout the lifespan. Many ethnic backgrounds, all types of personalities, and every form of relationship add to the richness and complexity of local churches. And if there are biases regarding class or gender, the Holy Spirit empowers the Word of God to challenge and change them.

The church is like a living organism, where the Trinity lives and breathes, awakening individuals to their full potential in Christ, stirring motivation that draws them forward, offering hope when difficulties overwhelm. Here pastoral counseling delivers the service of repair and recovery, providing confidential one-on-one or group sessions specifically designed to explore what troubles someone, what baffles or frustrates them, to the end that their lives are clarified and they are set on a path of healthy growth.

In a church counseling growth group I led, Charlie shared in halting words, face gaunt with pain, how he'd felt shunned by church members during the two years he and his wife Linda had attended the church.

"What makes you think that people have been judging you?" I asked.

"I was divorced before I married Linda. The pastor often preaches against divorce," he said, arms folded and legs locked together, reminding me of an armadillo encased behind armored plates.

"I see. So you've assumed that people in the church won't accept you because you've been divorced?"

"Exactly."

"And do you know this for sure?"

"Well, no one has been friendly toward us. Except maybe this group a little bit. That's why I'm mentioning it."

"I appreciate you sharing this issue with us. I wonder if you're open to hearing from people what they really think?"

He stiffened somewhat, yet nodded his assent.

Beckoning to the other eight persons in our circle, I said, "Out of curiosity, how many of you have known that Charlie was divorced before he married Linda?"

Only one hand went up, a woman named Barbara.

"Barbara," I said, "can you share how you came by this knowledge and how you felt about it?"

Barbara looked inquisitively at Linda, who gave a nod for Barbara to speak freely.

"Linda told me last year," said Barbara, "to help explain why Charlie holds back from people."

"And how did you handle the issue of his divorce?"

"I didn't think twice about it. I love them both and just wanted them to feel at home here. I tried being friendly to Charlie, but he didn't seem to notice."

"Thanks for sharing." I turned to Charlie. "Seems like no one but Barbara knew you were divorced, and she tried to show you her friendliness. What do you make of this?"

Charlie's face slackened. "It's new information. It never occurred to me I was reading people wrong."

It seemed time for a brief integration of psychology and spirituality. Addressing the group, I said, "The type of difficulty that Charlie got into happens to all of us, doesn't it. Our private perceptions influence how we believe others see us. If we have a negative experience, we can assume everyone sees us in that light, not knowing we're projecting our own negative bias onto them—even God has trouble convincing us that we're loveable. The interesting thing is, all we have to do is withdraw our negative projection and we can feel close to people again."

I noticed that Charlie was breathing more easily, his arms no longer tucked tightly over his chest. I turned toward him. "What are you feeling right now, Charlie?"

"Kind of amazed," he said. "I don't feel that wall between me and the people in this group any more. It makes me wonder if I haven't been hiding behind walls for years." He smiled as he looked around the circle. "This feels better."

With that the topic shifted to a new subject, and Charlie sat peacefully attentive, hearing from other people with a new look of caring on his face.

Psychology and The Word of God

The unique revelation of God in Jesus Christ, the Son sent by the Father to take away the sins of the world, reveals that Christianity's whole purpose centers on a proactive faith, inviting God's people to discover and actualize ever-greater depths of his love, peace, and joy.

While Scripture paints in bold strokes God's plan of salvation and the struggle between good and evil, the Bible was never meant as a handbook on personality theory or psychopathology. For that we need the information that behavioral science provides, just as God blesses humanity with the applied sciences of dentistry, optometry, and medicine.

Skilled pastoral counselors combine sound biblical principles with scientific psychology, bringing together a depth analysis of people's problems with an effective treatment strategy—a process that includes psychological as well as moral and spiritual dimensions.

My vision for developing pastoral counseling and coaching is two-fold:

1) To provide pastors and churches with a perspective on human growth that integrates trustworthy psychological principles with orthodox Christian faith, and helps pastors enjoy pastoral counseling.

2) To provide pastoral counselors with competent theory and techniques for therapeutic intervention across a wide range of human needs, while discerning when a referral to a licensed therapist is indicated.

Takeaways from this book include how to:

⊕ Integrate your identity as a pastoral counselor and coach with other skill-sets in pastoral ministry, making wise decisions for when parishioners need pastoral counseling or when they can be helped in other ways.

⊕ Discern the types of pastoral counseling such as brief situational support, short-term counseling, and long-term pastoral psychotherapy, and utilize what works best for you.

⊕ Apply the Human Nature Compass and Self Compass growth tools in adult education, preaching, and counseling sessions, to develop an overall church theme of helping people understand themselves in terms of Christ's own Self Compass and the interpersonal life of the Trinity.

As a prelude to presenting the Compass Therapy approach to pastoral counseling, here is a brief overview of the field that provides a definition, historical review, and explanation of the relationship of pastoral counseling to kindred fields.

Definition of Pastoral Counseling

Pastoral counseling involves a helping relationship between a religiously affiliated counselor and an individual, couple, or family who seek assistance for coping with life. Pastoral counselors include ordained ministers and consecrated professionals licensed in the field of counseling and therapy.

The word "pastoral" indicates that services are provided which are sensitive to the spiritual viewpoints and values of counselees regardless of their faith affiliation. A respect for the faith dimension of human experience is an important contribution of the pastoral counseling movement to the mental health field. Pastoral counseling assumes that a counselee's spiritual life has value in helping to heal emotional wounds, resolve conflicts, facilitate life transitions, and clarify values and purpose.

Pastoral counseling often takes the form of a specialized ministry within a church, where pastors or professional counselors offer pastoral counseling under the auspices of pastoral care. However, pastoral counseling can also function as an outreach ministry to a local hospital, homeless shelter, or independent counseling center; or it may serve persons through the chaplaincy in a prison, military base, or college campus.

I know of a pastor who has collaborated with the police department in his hometown for over twenty years. Early on they so valued his contributions that they gave him a badge with the title "Police Chaplain." Over the decades his phone has rung regularly for calls involving domestic disputes.

More typically, a pastoral counselor encounters a counselee who is grieving the loss of a loved one; a couple who need premarital counseling or help raising step-children; an individual addicted to substances; a person dealing with adverse work conditions; a parent overwhelmed by young children or adolescents; a family being torn apart by forces they don't understand; or a person searching for intimacy with God. By transforming broken personalities and reconciling damaged relationships, pastoral counseling helps persons and communities to become living expressions of God's redemptive love in the concreteness of daily life.

Most pastoral counselors have academic training in addition to religious credentials. These may include the Master of Divinity or Doctor of Ministry degrees, with a specialty in pastoral counseling. If a pastor has not had opportunity to study counseling in seminary, there are excellent Internet and external degree programs in pastoral counseling offered through credible institutions that strengthen competence in counseling.

On the other hand, some pastoral counselors meet with counselees on the basis of their religious credentials alone; Biblical counseling, for example, emphasizes helping parishioners respond to a crisis primarily through empathetic listening, prayer, and biblical instruction.

Consecrated mental health workers who work in religious settings or private practice are often licensed as psychologists, professional counselors, or marriage and family therapists. They may work in private practice or band together to form a church-based counseling center.

Pastoral Ministry

Pastoral ministry involves preaching, ecclesiastical, and worship dimensions of a religious community, drawing from pastoral counseling the principles that help promote spiritual and psychological growth in congregational care. Pastoral ministry enjoys the unique opportunity to participate in the lifespan development of parishioners, offering support through the passages of birth, baptism, marriage, childrearing, illness, and funerals. When pastoral ministers observe significant signs of unresolved stress in someone's life, they can suggest the benefits of pastoral counseling. And if the pastoral minister does pastoral counseling, there is a depth dimension that accrues from overseeing people's congregational life, while helping them individually through difficult times.

Applied Theology

Applied theology, also termed "practical theology," is a more recent development in Christian ministry. This field translates the theology and dogma of Christianity into personalized delivery systems, including marriage enrichment, divorce recovery, the handling of stress, anxiety, or depression, spearheading just solutions to community problems, the healing of painful memories, or the development of supportive cell groups aimed at meeting interpersonal needs. Applied theology intersects with pastoral counseling in many creative ways to help hurting people become more whole.

Psychology of Religion

Psychology of religion is an academic field, often housed in secular universities, that builds upon William James' exploration of the varieties of religious experience common to humankind (1902). By promoting both research and philosophical inquiry into the psychological dynamics of religious traditions, a synthesis of faith and reason results in interpretative paradigms that influence contemporary religious life and help ensure the promotion of psychological and spiritual health.

Spiritual Direction

Spiritual direction, a method of mentorship used over the centuries, brings together a seasoned veteran of religious life with an individual who seeks insights, encouragement, and dialogue. Topics may include how to better understand one's self, find reconciliation with others, and know God more personally. When intrapsychic or interpersonal problems of a substantive nature emerge, a spiritual director does well to recommend pastoral counseling.

Pastoral Psychotherapy

Pastoral psychotherapy offers services of a more intense therapeutic nature, requiring academic and supervisory experience on the part of the pastoral counselor, and state licensure if the pastoral counselor is also a mental health professional. There is relatively less reliance upon religious tradition and proportionately more utilization of empirically validated methods of treatment to effect personality reconstruction. Since pastoral psychotherapy represents a longer and more intensive relationship with the counselee, psychodynamic factors come into play such as transference and counter-transference, family of origin dynamics, secondary gains from illness, the disruptive power of personality disorders, the meaning of dreams, and the role of the unconscious in symptom formation as well as transformative healing.

Compass Psychotheology

Compass Psychotheology anchors a Christian personality theory within the Triune God, suggesting that the foundation of human personhood is the eternal personhood of God, and asserting that the source of the universal need for love and belonging echoes the love and belonging that the Father, Son, and Holy Spirit share for one another and for every human being.

An Alliance for Healing and Growth

Taken together, pastoral counseling, pastoral ministry, applied theology, the psychology of religion, spiritual direction, pastoral psychotherapy, and compass psychotheology deliver spiritual and psychological resources that strengthen persons, families, and communities.

I invite you to envision with me the Father, Son, and Holy Spirit's empowering of pastoral counselors in the twenty-first century, serving the needs of churches and communities, representing the healing love of God-with-us.

2. Pastoral Counseling Comes of Age

Who has come before you? Who has contributed to your identity and vision as a pastoral counselor?

Contributors to Pastoral Care and Counseling

Though pastoral counseling has existed for millennia in the form of "caring for the soul," its expression today relates to the development of psychological counseling theories in the twentieth and twenty-first centuries. Many pastoral counseling pioneers intuitively integrated principles of psychology and counseling with their understanding of God and faith, scripture and doctrine, and the varieties of religious experience among their counselees.

Psychologist William James, one of the first American thinkers to envision the integration of behavioral science and religious faith, wrote *Varieties of Religious Experience* (1902) to place this topic on the agenda for future exploration in universities, churches, and seminaries.

Influential contributors to the history and diversity of pastoral counseling include, among others, Seward Hiltner, Paul Johnson, Anton Boisen, Carroll Wise, Howard Clinebell, Wayne Oates, Jay Adams, Lawrence Crabb, Richard Dayringer, David Brenner, Gary Collins, John MacArthur,

Rodney Hunter, Nancy Ramsay, Donald Capps, Robert Wicks, Howard Stone, Pamela Cooper-White, James Dittes, Carrie Doehring, Jeanne Stevenson-Messner, Ray S. Anderson, Deborah Van Deusen Hunsinger, Dan Montgomery, Raymond Pendleton, Abigail Rian Evans, David Augsburger, Ann Ulanov, and H. Newton Malony.

Beginning in the early twentieth century, pioneering pastors and priests began to integrate Freudian, Jungian, and Adlerian theories with their experiences in pastoral care. The aftermath of World War II provided a major impetus in the United States for the use of psychology by pastors, particularly through the development of Clinical Pastoral Education taught in interdisciplinary programs through colleges and universities.

Seward Hiltner (University of Chicago), discerning the rich connection between religion and mental health, wrote the influential book *Pastoral Counseling* (1949). Carroll Wise (Garrett) focused on the application of psychoanalytic theory in church counseling. Paul Johnson (Boston University) emphasized "responsive" counseling, drawing from Harry Stack Sullivan's interpersonal theory. Wayne Oates (Southern Baptist Theological Seminary) sought to give pastoral counseling full standing in medical school training and chaplaincy programs.

The American Association of Pastoral Counselors (AAPC) was founded in 1963 with Howard Clinebell as its first president. In his classic *Basic Types of Pastoral Counseling* (1966), Clinebell helped consolidate the field of pastoral counseling, advocating that pastoral counselors complement their ministerial credentials with competent training in psychological counseling theories.

Perhaps in reaction to this emphasis, Thomas Oden, fearing that pastoral counselors might err in becoming pseudopsychologists instead of pastoral caregivers, encouraged the incorporation of pre-modern psychologies and traditional forms of spirituality in pastoral counseling (1983).

Charles Gerkin (1984) developed the theology of providence in relation to crisis experiences, presenting the pastoral counselor as a skilled "interpreter," assisting the integration a counselee's life story within their larger faith tradition. Similarly, John Patton emphasized the pastoral counselor's use of "relational humanness" in dealing with issues of guilt, shame, and forgiveness (1985).

The most ecumenical expression of pastoral counseling, the *Dictionary of Pastoral Care and Counseling* by Rodney Hunter and Nancy Ramsay (1996; 2005), enlisted the participation of nearly 600 Protestant, Catholic, Orthodox, and Jewish contributors.

Pastoral Counseling Contrasted to Secular Therapy

Today there is unparalleled interest in pastoral counseling, both among professionals called to this field and among those many people interested in receiving it. Jews, Christians, Moslems, Hindus, Buddhists, and other spiritual seekers often prefer a counselor of their same "faith-family" as a trusted resource in time of need.

What distinguishes pastoral counseling from secular therapy is the expectation that the pastoral counselor is qualified to address not only psychological but spiritual needs. These spiritual needs include finding a meaningful relationship with God; handling inner conflicts between guilt and grace; discussing categories of good and evil; exploring issues regarding salvation and the afterlife; discussing angelic protection or demonic oppression; finding support during illness; grieving over the death of a loved one; seeking purpose and security in an anxiety-ridden world; and longing to transform self-confusion into wholeness and holiness.

While the pastoral counselor shares with the secular mental health professional a concern for what best serves the wellbeing of counselees and helps to resolve their presenting problems, the pastoral counselor enjoys unique ethical permission to utilize religious resources, rituals, and sacraments that transcend the boundaries of scientific psychology. An extraordinary gift that pastoral counselors can offer counselees, which is not a prerogative for psychiatrists or psychologists, is a prayer of blessing from God or a discerning word from Scripture.

Contributions of Therapeutic Psychology

Insights from the field of therapeutic psychology have greatly enriched pastoral counseling. From Sigmund Freud (1920) came descriptions of the major ego-defense mechanisms, vital in helping counselees understand how they might be resisting the very truth that can heal them. These include rationalization, denial, projection, reaction formation, repression, intellectualization, passive-aggression, and acting out.

Carl Jung (1933) viewed faith in God as an essential dimension of mental health, saying, "I don't believe God exists. I *know* God exists." He reported that most of his patients in the second half of life were deeply concerned with religious issues, and helped us understand that symbols, whether in the form of dreams or daydreams, can carry religious meaning about discerning God's will for one's spiritual pathway.

Viktor Frankl (1946) bore witness, through his survival of a Nazi death camp, that even in the most tragic of circumstances, persons retain a degree of freedom to choose their inner attitudes. He called the search for meaning a universal spiritual and psychological quest.

Erik Erikson (1950) developed the concept of eight stages of life, suggesting that a successful resolution of these life crises gives birth to the life-affirming virtues of hope, will, purpose, competence, fidelity, love, caring, and wisdom.

Rollo May (1965) viewed the goal of pastoral counseling as increasing a person's freedom, spontaneity, and genuineness. He described the counseling process as offering counselees "the grace of clarification" to release them from the anguish of egocentricity.

Carl Rogers (1965) recognized the importance of prizing the counselee. His work as a consultant to Seward Hiltner focused early formulations of pastoral counseling in the direction of developing warmth, congruence, and unconditional positive regard in the pastoral counselor's therapeutic style.

Thomas Harris (1967) popularized the work of psychiatrist Eric Berne, calling this approach to counseling Transactional Analysis, providing pastoral counselors with practical insights into the Parent, Adult, and Child ego states of their counselees.

Aaron Beck (1975) noted that what people are thinking directly influences the emotions they feel, and that cognitive assumptions about life need constant revision in order to become healthy and adaptive rather than self-defeating. Many pastoral counselors benefited by adding elements of Cognitive Therapy to their approaches.

My colleague Everett Shostrom and I suggested that self-actualizing in relation to God is a reasonable goal of pastoral counseling (1978). Further, we put forward the concept that counseling involves the whole of human nature: cognition and emotion, sensation and spirituality (1986).

Twenty-first Century Pastoral Counseling Comes of Age

The rejuvenation of pastoral counseling in both church and community is shown by the abundance of church-based counseling centers and the extensive Internet offerings of pastoral counseling educational resources. Most denominations are encouraging their ministers to develop pastoral counseling skill-sets that enrich their pastoral care.

Seminaries are strengthening their offerings in pastoral psychology and counseling, including programs for the Christian, Jewish, Islamic, Buddhist, and Hindu faiths. Chaplaincy programs apply principles of pastoral counseling to enhance preparedness for service in hospitals, prisons, the military, and university campuses.

The rise of the Psychology of Religion Division within the American Psychological Association underscores the prestige of pastoral counseling as contributing valuable principles to the mental health field—namely, for working with the universal spiritual needs of humankind.

An ever-growing assortment of journals and books specifically relating to pastoral counseling and pastoral psychology stimulate and nourish the worldwide development of indigenous pastoral counselors serving church and society.

3. THREE TYPES OF PASTORAL COUNSELING

Understandably, the pastoral counseling experience requires a counselee's protection from pressures of indoctrination or proselytizing. While the pastoral counselor remains free to utilize religious resources and prayer when these contribute to a counselee's personal growth, respect must be shown for the counselee's own value system, which may or may not be religiously oriented.

Thus a pastoral counselor shows a comparable sensitivity to the perceptual field of a Catholic, Protestant, Hindu, Buddhist, Islamic, Jewish, New Age, agnostic, or atheistic counselee. An open-ended curiosity about other religions is helpful—coupled with listening to the counselee's innermost concerns. I think of this as bracketing out one's own value system in favor of forming a therapeutic alliance that shows humility, empathy, and resourcefulness regarding the counselee's presenting problems.

It's not that you forget who you are or what you believe, but that you have enough security in your personal identity to make room for a person different from you. Perhaps this is akin to what God offers humanity by giving room for individual differences within the scope of the Trinity's love. A side benefit of pastoral counseling lies in how other people's stories expand the boundaries of our own perspectives.

Depending on the training and orientation of the pastoral counselor, there are three levels of counseling that can interface with the particular needs of a counselee. These include brief situational support, short-term counseling, and long-term pastoral psychotherapy.

Brief Situational Support

Brief situational support consists of one to three sessions aimed at strengthening counselees in life situations that have temporarily thrown them off course.

Let's say a woman comes to you feeling stunned and confused because her husband died that weekend. Relatives are arriving from out-of-town to assist with the funeral. She tells you through tears that she doesn't know how to act around them. Then she bites her lip, as though apologetic for her show of emotion.

"Andrea," you say, "it's okay to let your feelings come out here. Let yourself breathe and say whatever comes to you."

Here you are defining the counseling encounter as a safe place to contact emotions and let them pass through her. You are showing that while you are in charge of the session, she is free to express herself spontaneously. You are also implying trust in her, that as she discharges emotions and catches up with her thoughts, she will find a way through this situation.

After looking pensive for a minute, during which you relax your body and respectfully await her next communication, she takes a deep breath and says, "Should I be brave and make everyone comfortable? Or should I just cry when I feel how much I miss Brad?"

You explore this and find that her heart is aching terribly over the loss of her husband. She can barely even conceive of life without him. Yet she needs a way to behave in the midst of her many relatives.

"It's like you are torn between concentrating on your feelings of loss and trying to watch after your visitors. Is that right?"

Asking if your interpretation is on track lets counselees focus even more clearly on what they are experiencing. If they agree with you they will automatically move forward. If they disagree, they will add the nuance of thought or feeling that provides greater detail.

"Exactly," she says. "I'm trying to make sure people have enough to eat and somewhere to sleep, and then suddenly I feel like I've been hit in the chest with a two-by-four."

Now you want to expand the emotion behind the chest metaphor so that she can literally get the pressure off her chest.

"This deep emotion about Brad...what name would you give it?"

Her eyes grow distant, as though lost in thought. Then her shoulders slump and she sighs from her depths. "I feel...lost. Like there's no 'me' inside me. Like I have tunnel vision and feel numb all over."

"This is perfectly understandable, Andrea. You are in shock. And your body is temporarily shutting down in order to protect you until you have time to sort things out."

She tears up, a good sign that you've said the right thing, for her expression is no longer simply blank, but rather conveys the relief of expressing a core feeling and being understood.

Aware that the session time is nearly over, you offer a tentative suggestion. "Do you suppose it might work this week to go ahead and say when you're feeling overwhelmed, so that you're taking care of yourself as well as interacting with your relatives?"

Closing her eyes, she nods. "Yes, I think that's what I need to do."

Notice in this counseling transaction the sense of forward movement, even to the point of offering a creative plan. Counselees need more than having their feelings accepted; they need ideas to consider, perspectives to try on for size, tentative plans that steer them in a productive direction. In brief situational support the coaching dimension of pastoral counseling provides these elements. You close the session with prayer, inviting Andrea to come back if she needs further support.

Other situations appropriate for brief situational support might include talking with a college student who is so homesick he's considering dropping out of school; brainstorming with a counselee who has lost his job and feels submerged in a whirlpool of failure feelings; or comforting a woman who confides that she's gone through the motions of religion for years without ever feeling close to God.

Brief situational support occurs most often within the faith community and reflects the heart-pulse of pastoral counseling and coaching. When parishioners speak transparently to a pastor, a church becomes a home. Pastoral counseling in this context helps to stabilize, nurture, guide, inspire, and lend a helping hand.

The mere availability of pastoral counseling helps people feel the presence of a safety net underneath them, as the Psalmist recognized when he wrote: "Underneath are the everlasting arms."

Long before I embarked on my counseling career I had a single session with a gifted pastoral counselor. I described how awkward I felt around people and how my way of emotionally blurting things out often backfired.

"So it seems like your impulsive style of speaking works against you more than you'd like," he said.

"Yes," I replied, amazed at the warmth that his eyes conveyed. "And I'm afraid that not even God can change me."

He folded his hands together and looked thoughtful. Then he exhaled slowly and said, "Dan, I think the Lord is giving me a visual picture about you. If I understand it correctly, I see you as a boulder in a river filled with rapids. While you may seem rugged right now, in due time the Holy Spirit is going to rub off and polish your rough edges. I believe that someday you're going to become a rock of support who helps other people know that God loves them."

That visual metaphor has traveled with me these forty years. I hope I've become a source of God's love to others as much as that pastoral counselor was for me.

Contemporary models that can strengthen your capability for providing brief situational support are found in books like: *Strategies in Brief Pastoral Counseling*, by Howard Stone (2001); *Counseling: How to Counsel Biblically*, by John MacArthur (2005); and *Christian Counseling: An Introduction* (2007), by H. Newton Malony and David Augsburger.

Short-term Pastoral Counseling

Short-term pastoral counseling usually requires four to nine sessions in order to move through the therapeutic cycle of problem analysis, experimentation with coping strategies, and consolidation of gains. More time is taken for exploration of the presenting problem, a review of the person's history—especially as it bears on the issues at hand—and the mobilization of a treatment plan to help counselees make progress toward agreed-upon goals.

Ronnie, a man of forty, reports his frustration with dating relationships that end abruptly after several months. During the first phase of counseling you build rapport with him, asking open-ended questions about his upbringing, exploring his high school dating experience, and discussing the failed relationships that have checkered his adult life. A pattern emerges. You find out that he had a smothering mother who dominated him, and a father who never stood up to the mother on his behalf. You realize that not only did Ronnie never receive good modeling on how to relate to the female gender, but he also developed a fair amount of unconscious anger toward his mother's controlling ways.

In the middle phase of counseling you share in a gentle manner your working hypothesis that Ronnie lets women get very close to him, like his mother was, because it feels familiar and offers comfort; then he suddenly panics because he feels like they have become invasive and smothering. He wants to tell them off to re-establish his self-boundaries, but because he was never allowed to express anger, he resolves the problem by terminating the relationship, only to be left all alone again. Because you are offering these insights only as he ratifies them, his consciousness is raised to the point where after a fifth session, he risks starting a relationship with someone new.

In the final phase of counseling, and as a consequence of your coaching him about diplomatic assertion, Ronnie reports that he is replacing his old passive-aggressive tendency with a new openness to talk to his woman friend about their communication. He says he feels ready to proceed on his own. You congratulate him on his progress, suggest a book to help strengthen his relational skills, and invite him to return for a future visit if he wants a "tune-up."

Short-term pastoral counseling and coaching might work well with the father who's having communication and discipline problems with his teenage son; the overly shy business person who wants to develop more ease around people; the husband and wife who have lost their sexual connection; or the missionary who has pioneered several churches yet secretly feels unloved by God.

Established models for doing short-term pastoral counseling are described in these books: *Strategic Pastoral Counseling: A Short-Term Structured Model*, by David Benner (2003); *Christian Counseling That Really Works*, by Dan Montgomery (2006); and *Christian Counseling: A Comprehensive Guide*, by Gary Collins (2007).

Long-term Pastoral Psychotherapy

Long-term pastoral psychotherapy generally requires ten sessions to a year or more. While some exposure to clinical pastoral training is recommended for all pastoral counselors, long-term pastoral psychotherapy in particular needs formal academic and supervisory training in the field of counseling.

If brief situational counseling is like taking a car in for lubrication, oil change, and tire rotation, then longer term pastoral psychotherapy is like rebuilding the car's engine. This requires the thorough integration of a Christian personality theory with a well-established counseling theory, and supervision of your initial counseling experience. You want enough knowledge about personality disorders to treat counselees with narcissistic, compulsive, paranoid, antisocial, histrionic, dependent, avoidant, schizoid, and borderline personality patterns. You want enough knowledge of biochemical disorders such as chronic depression, bipolar disorder, and attention-deficit disorder to discern when a referral for medical evaluation is indicated. You want an understanding of the role of the unconscious in the generation of psychopathology and the therapeutic transformation of personality. And you will undergo a course of psychotherapeutic treatment yourself, a standard requirement for advanced degrees in counseling, so that your own personality patterns do not negatively impact the counseling process.

The reason for this extensive psychological preparation is simply that you don't want the counselee to become worse off for seeing you! And this is what can happen when a counselee's repressed emotions, irrational thoughts, conflicted values, and pent-up pain enter the counseling arena. You can take them too far too fast, or make a seemingly innocuous remark that sets in motion rash decisions, suicidal urges, destructive aggression, or the collapse of a fragile sense of self.

Nor do you want to become emotionally enmeshed with your counselee, so that you both topple off the nearest cliff. Think of it like this: if your counselee needs you as a guide to ascend Mount Everest, you want to have safely guided many people up that mountain so that you know the territory.

That said, pastoral psychotherapy contributes profoundly to the present and future wellbeing of people that it serves, for it can transform barriers to wholeness, creating a positive behavioral legacy that will bless generations of people to come. You just have to know that you are called to this vocation and that you have acquired the expertise to deliver on its challenges.

Contemporary theoretical and practical tools for the empowerment of pastoral psychotherapy are found in the following books: *Pastoral Counseling and Personality Disorders*, by Richard Vaughan (1994); *Clinical Handbook of Pastoral Counseling*, edited by Robert Wicks, Richard Parsons, and Donald Capps (2003); and *Compass Therapy: Christian Psychology In Action*, by Dan Montgomery (2008).

I suggest that if you have a passion for counseling, you set about developing your capability in all three types of pastoral counseling—brief, short-term, and long-term—so that you can exercise wisdom and creativity in meeting a wide range of counselee needs, enjoying the freedom and fulfillment this brings you.

Now let's begin to apply the central models of Compass Therapy to pastoral counseling and coaching: the *Human Nature Compass* (Part Two) and the *Self Compass* growth tool (Part Three).

4. Setting Up A First Session

Let's speculate a little, for the purpose of enhancing empathy with counselees, about what goes on within a person before making a first contact with a pastoral counselor.

It's awful when individuals feel bound up with a knotty life problem that won't go away and doesn't get better, no matter what efforts they make, no matter what advice they receive from trusted friends, the problem even defying heartfelt prayer, a sense of helplessness accruing alongside inner anxiety.

It may be that a third child, unlike the first two who were calm and sociable, climbs the walls day and night, paying no attention to parental pleas or reprimands. Or it may be that sexual issues have come to haunt the marriage bed. Or what about a person who has recurring anxiety attacks and doesn't know why?

Every counselee feels anguish. They would not contact you if pain and perplexity didn't compel them. And once they are resolved to reach out, there is the added uncertainty about how you will respond to them.

Kushner and Sher (1991) say this *treatment fearfulness* is commonly underestimated by counselors, but nevertheless acts as a genuine obstacle in seeking help. Further, Shay (1996) has observed that men especially may have some culturally determined resistance to counseling because of the intimate sharing it requires. Take heart, though. Research shows that counselees have a greater probability of experiencing healing in their area of need than do patients who seek a physician's care (Wampold, 2003). And, generally speaking, the more anxious and distressed people are when they enter counseling, the more likely they will continue with it and the more benefit they are apt to derive (Greencavage & Norcross, 1990). Keep in mind, too, that many people prefer seeing a counselor who is sensitive to spiritual values over one who is secular-minded.

Fears and all, then, many hurting persons reach a point where they decide to pursue pastoral counseling, mustering the courage to make a first contact. They may know you from church, hear of your work from someone you've counseled, or find your site on the Internet. In their moment of reaching out, a touch of hope stirs within them, a warranted hope, since God is encouraging them to make a counseling connection with you.

Now, for our part, what goes on inside us to prepare for a first session with a new counselee? Personally, I am helped by an open-ended prayer conversation that says to the Lord, "Please send me only those individuals that in your providence you want me to see, and please guide us from beginning to end." This steadies my confidence in God's superintendence of my counseling practice, helping my unconscious to accept that the Lord is guiding people long before they see me, and will continue to help them long after our counseling is over. I want God's multifaceted involvement in my counseling and coaching practice. After all, Christ is the one who originally called me to this profession!

Another way of preparing for new counselees is simply not scheduling more appointments than you can handle in a given week. This means diplomatically saying "no" to a prospective counselee who would create an overload in your counseling practice: "I'm very sorry but my practice is full just now. Let me give you a few names of other counselors who might be able to see you." This is hard for me, since I want to help every person who needs me, and, at a less mature level, I am flattered when people call upon my expertise.

The tendency to overbook threatens the delicate balance of a healthy pastoral counseling practice. Seeing too many people—even one too many counselees—leaves us irritable or exhausted after a day of counseling. This in turn deprives spouses and children of rightful energy needed to nourish them. It doesn't take long for a spouse to think, "My husband (or wife) cares more about taking care of other people than about me!"

I suggest placing your spouse at the top of the list of those who need nurturing love. An intimate marriage deepens the reservoir of energy required for serving counselees effectively. If you are single, this overload appears more as a secret depression: like being crushed under a heavy load that no one else knows about. Either way, you learn to place your physical and psychological wellbeing as a primary priority, recognizing that by showing this love for yourself, you'll have energy to care for others.

In either case, watch out for the isolation that comes with over-exposure to counselees. Counter this isolation with the development of hobbies and social outings that keep you interested in life and rejuvenate your spirit. You want longevity, not burnout. I know. I've burned out twice over three decades. Each time it took several months free from counseling to recover my health, identity, and sense of enjoyment of this challenging vocation.

Handling the First Contact

There are several ways a potential counselee can make contact: by e-mail, phone, or perhaps calling you aside at a church activity for a quick conversation. Let's deal with these in order.

E-mail communications are perilous. They are insecure because you have no control over who might get hold of them in cyberspace, or who might read the potential counselee's e-mail, including an irate spouse or a future attorney.

It works fine to post an e-mail address alongside your website, if this is how you want to reach out to the church or community. But here is a creative way to instruct people on how to use it: "Feel free to contact me by e-mail to set up a free phone consultation. At that time I will evaluate your situation and answer questions you might have; then, if you so choose, we'll schedule a first appointment."

When you speak together on the phone, spend fifteen or twenty minutes exploring the presenting problem and then move into a summary of what they've told you and how you'll proceed in a first working session. Don't get sidetracked by allowing the phone consult to turn into a therapeutic intervention. And don't get trapped into offering premature assessments, as when a wife says, "Do you think my husband can ever get over his angry outbursts?" In this instance you could say, "Many people change negative behaviors into positive ones, but the choice is up to them."

During the phone consult don't let the person blurt out a life story filled with emotion and excessive details. Rather, break in regularly to focus the conversation on eliciting information that helps you determine whether this is an appropriate counselee for your particular practice. Ask yourself these kinds of questions. "What are the psychological and spiritual dynamics of this problem?" "How long has the problem persisted?" "Is this a situational conflict that seems resolvable, or does it sound like a personality disorder is driving the problem?" (More about personality patterns and disorders are covered in Part Three). "Have other counselors been involved or am I the first?" "Will treating an issue like this most likely take five or fifteen or fifty sessions?" "Is this person stable enough to respond to my preferred style of pastoral counseling?" "How comfortable and competent do I feel handling this person's area of need?"

I know this amounts to processing a lot of information during the course of a brief conversation with a total stranger, but with time and practice, such self-dialogue becomes second nature. There's no perfect way to screen people for possible counseling; no protocol that you can memorize mechanically. You simply develop your own creative method of covering the preliminary territory and keep refining it until you are fairly comfortable talking extemporaneously to most people regarding prospective counseling.

Another way for a potential counselee to contact you is by striking up a conversation at church. Actually, some people will sit beside you at a church dinner, or call you aside in the corridor to ask a quick question, all the while deciding within themselves if they want to see you in a counseling context.

Keep in mind that you don't have to sell anyone on the idea of entering counseling with you, and that they need a certain level of genuine motivation to make counseling worthwhile. This leads to a paradox: pastoral counseling in a religious community can be both fulfilling and exasperating. It is fulfilling because you see individuals, couples, and extended families develop over the years, and provide assistance when they are experiencing unusual stress or confusion. In this way, you are serving the Body of Christ through a gift of the Holy Spirit—pastoral counseling—that fulfills your call to watch over the congregation.

On the other hand, certain people can take advantage of this situation by buttonholing you and dumping a huge amount of personal emotion and information in your lap, then walking off because they have no intention of changing themselves or their attitudes.

My personal guideline is to keep casual conversations with people at church socials at a casual level. This way I can enjoy the conversations without putting on my counseling hat. But if I realize that this person is not only unburdening themselves to me, but also reaching out for help that can come through a pastoral counseling connection, I may shift the conversation to suggesting that an office visit with me or another professional counselor might be in order. After making that suggestion, I will leave them completely free to decide, but I will pull back from going deeper into their issue because they really do need the context and focus of a counseling session in order to make real progress.

The Countenance of a Counselor

The first impression a counselee will receive from you, and the impression that may stay with them for some time, lies in whether you are warm and personable—not casual and unprofessional, mind you, but simply human and accessible. While attorneys and surgeons may have the option of being cool and remote, pastoral counselors do not.

Everything rests on your counselee's sense of whether or not they can open up to you, whether you are trustworthy or not, whether you prize them or not. I remember watching Carl Rogers counseling a volunteer counselee at a weekend workshop. It wasn't what he said that moved me, as much as how humanly present he was with this woman. There was the hint of a smile on his face and in his voice, even though he was conveying thoughtful reflection about what she said to him. I thought to myself, "Dan, you've got to lighten up with your own counselees. You're too poker-faced. You've got to convey more warmth." Indeed, I had been trained at the University of New Mexico that counseling and psychotherapy is a serious profession, and that by giving counselees a look of objective neutrality throughout the session I would help them to concentrate on their inner material. It took years to get over that aspect of my training, and to replace that blank look with facial expressions that flowed from whatever the counselee was confiding.

Carl Rogers, Virginia Satir, Rollo May, and other master counselors whom I've observed in person helped me discover that good counseling involves human-to-human communication. Inspirational teachers and coaches know this. They're not afraid to greet you with a smile, pat you on the back when you've achieved something significant, or frown when they are perplexed. So when you invite each counselee into your office, enjoy giving a warm smile and a firm handshake. This sends the message: "I respect your courage to come in for counseling; now, how can I help you out?"

Your Body Language Matters

While we're on the topic of a counselor's body language, let me mention three more cues. Watch your hands the next time you are counseling. Make sure they are not fidgeting or locked together in an ironclad grip. Use selective relaxation to connect the occasional smile you offer during a session with a relaxed pair of hands. Then look at your legs. Is one of your feet bobbing up and down like a cork in water?

Mouth, hands, legs, feet: all are visual cues that convey attention or inattention to your counselee. Opt for a relaxed body in which you are breathing easily and making natural gestures when you speak. This conveys relational connection. Beyond this, you can use the style of communication with which you are accustomed. Some counselors have a dramatic and histrionic style. Others are more calm and composed. This is fine. But do become aware of your body language so that you can maintain an accurate picture of how the counselee is seeing you.

The First Working Session

Considerable evidence has accrued to demonstrate that the more positive the attitudes and expectations with which counselees enter and pursue counseling, the more likely they are to make therapeutic gains. A first working session sets the tone for the counseling in so many ways that it is worth examining more closely.

A reliable opening statement may go like this:

"Well, Rick, I'm glad you found my office okay. Now I wonder if you might tell me what brings you here."

"Do I start at the beginning or with what happened last week?"

"Just say whatever is on your mind. It won't be long before you're giving me a good picture of what's going on."

(Here I am giving general permission to say anything that comes to mind during the counseling process. This is like the psychoanalytic rule of free association to whatever enters the counselee's consciousness, holding nothing back, no matter how seemingly insignificant).

Rick warms me up to his situation and I ask open-ended questions that start with "how," "what," "who," "where," and "when" rather than "why." This is because "why" questions like "why did you say that to the man," often lead to conversational dead-ends like, "Just because."

Questions that call for description or discovery naturally generate new information. "What did you feel when your father used to give you those long, angry lectures?" "How did you cope with your feelings of sadness and insecurity?" "Who did you hang out with when you felt all pent-up inside and just wanted to get things off your chest?" "Where did you go after graduating from high school?"

Also, when a counselee gives a vague, nondescript answer like, "I just felt weird a lot," you can ask, "How do you mean?" Then the counselee will search for other words to elaborate.

(I continue with Rick). "So I'm curious about the way you would take out your anger against your dad by riding your motorcycle fast. How did that work?"

"Well, it was really weird, but I'd stomp out and ride like crazy."

"How do you mean?"

"I mean I'd get pissed off and drive my bike at ninety on the freeway, right smack in the downdraft of some big semi."

"And how did this connect with your dad? Was it like winning a contest against him?"

"No. It was like punching him in the face because he hated me riding fast."

In a first session, you want to build a free-flowing conversation with the counselee for the first third of the session, and then in the mid-portion formulate agreed-upon goals. Be sure and leave enough time in the last third of the session to deal with questionnaires and consent forms, or whatever you need to administer your practice.

Zeroing In On Agreed-Upon Counseling Goals

Here is a glimpse into the mid-portion of the first session with Rick.

"I'm beginning to understand how your childhood conflicts with your father created hurt and anger that have followed you into adult life. Is that right?"

"Exactly," says Rick. "I think that's why I get into arguments with my boss. I don't take criticism well."

"So would you like to make better peace with your Dad and build new skills for interacting with your boss?"

"That sounds good, as long as I don't sell out."

"How do you mean?"

"If we're not talking about making me into a weenie."

"Here's where a tool called the Self Compass will help us. We can strengthen your diplomatic assertion even while helping you relax around authority figures."

"Okay. I can go for that."

Providing Assessment Tools & Consent Form

Now we move into the last segment of the first session, where the executive function of a counselor takes charge to accomplish certain tasks.

"Very good. Now, I'm going to give you a packet to take home with you. The first item you see is this *Multimodal Life History Inventory* (I pull it out and flip through the pages). Answer all the questions that you want to because it gives me valuable information about your thoughts, feelings, sensations, and spirituality. Most people enjoy doing this and it gives me a lot of information right away."

(This streamlined inventory was developed years ago by my colleague Arnold Lazarus to generate a considerable amount of information for the counselor, while encouraging counselees to specify their goals. It is available online through Research Press).

"Nobody sees this but you, right?"

"Right. Counseling information is confidential, just like it is when we're talking. Next, I'd like you to complete this personality assessment (I pull it out and explain how to take it). Bring it back to our next session. It will generate insight into your personality and relationships that is valuable to us" (Speaking in this inclusive manner builds our therapeutic alliance).

"What's this last one?"

"It's the 'Consent to Counseling Form' that explains pastoral counseling and gives me permission to be your counselor. Go ahead and read it. I'll answer any questions; then sign it and we're done for today."

He does so. I take the consent form for my files, give him the packet with questionnaire and assessment, and ask when he would like to schedule our next session.

On the way out I shake his hand. "It's a pleasure working with you, Rick. See you next week."

Assessment Considerations

What you select in terms of an assessment battery is entirely up to you, and reflects your academic training, supervised experience, and type of pastoral counseling elected for a particular counselee. For instance, in offering brief situational support there is little need for a life history inventory or personality assessment. By the same token, the Human Nature Compass and Self Compass that I explain in this book will help you quickly size up the presenting problem, intuitively grasp the psychodynamics of the counselee, and build an effective growth strategy.

Additionally, for short-term counseling you might choose a simple personality instrument like the *Taylor Johnson Temperament Analysis* or *Myers-Briggs Type Indicator*. For long-term pastoral psychotherapy, however, you'll definitely want a powerful instrument like the *Millon Clinical Multiaxial Inventory* that picks up personality disorders and other forms of psychopathology.

At any rate, keep in mind that you want to enjoy meeting any new counselee for the first time, opening the door of your mind to hear their fascinating life narrative, joining together with God and the counselee to form a healing partnership that helps transform their difficulties into creative ways of living and coping.

Part II: The Human Nature Compass

5. APPLYING THE HUMAN NATURE COMPASS

If I could pass on to you one conceptual tool that would illuminate your work with every future counselee, I would choose the Human Nature Compass. Consider for a moment how all people hold in common a human nature with which God has endowed Homo sapiens. Regardless of age, gender, culture, religion, socioeconomic status, or educational level, human nature contains the same elements.

In Christianity, unique among world religions, human nature takes on new meaning. Jesus of Nazareth, fully God and fully human, takes human nature into the Godhead. Jesus lays aside his divinity enough to encompass corporeal reality, to think and feel and sense and pray the way every human being learns to do.

Not only does the Son of God become the Son of Man, but he lives the whole of his life on earth with the same dependency upon the Father and the Holy Spirit that we are called to know. This is profound because it means that Jesus didn't cheat; he didn't have an extraordinary advantage over his brothers and sisters on earth, but rather felt hungry and thirsty like we do, knew pain and suffering like we know, felt anxiety and anger in exasperating situations, and was overcome by temporary feelings of despair, desperation, and even estrangement from God before he died. Is it any wonder, then, that Christ, now present to creation in the fullness of his Trinitarian reign, cares diligently and deeply about those persons whose human nature gives them trouble?

Understanding the dynamics of human nature increases your effectiveness with every counselee you see.

The Nature of Human Nature

While theologians may debate what constitutes human nature, the pastoral counselor needs a working model that brings x-ray vision for seeing into the counselee's very being.

Many theological debates have revolved around whether God created humans with a bipartite nature (body and soul) or a tripartite nature (spirit, mind, and body). However the diverse ways in which the Bible refers to the human person include such varied elements as body, soul, spirit, mind, and heart.

Perhaps the bipartite and tripartite conceptions reflect Greek dualism more than the biblical holism presented in Scripture (Berkouwer, 1962). There's a sense in the biblical narrative that human nature is a unity with contributing elements. We need to formulate this into a holistic model well-suited for pastoral counseling, a model that avoids dualism and doesn't fragment a person into part eternal substance (soul and spirit) and part temporal substance (body, mind, and heart).

Compass Therapy, with its intrinsic interest in uniting polar opposites into compass-like wholes, proposes a solution. Just as a physical compass places the compass points of north and south, east and west into a circle, so too the Compass model employs the multilevel framework of Mind (cognition) and Heart (emotion), Body (biology) and Spirit (purpose) into the understanding of human nature.

The Human Nature Compass is especially useful in pastoral counseling because it enables you to observe and engage a counselee's whole being, while monitoring how each part is functioning in relation to the whole. Mind stands for cognitive thinking. Heart expresses emotive feeling. Body emphasizes biological senses. Spirit describes values and purpose. The core is the innermost dimension of the person that has the power of self-reflection, and can say, "I am."

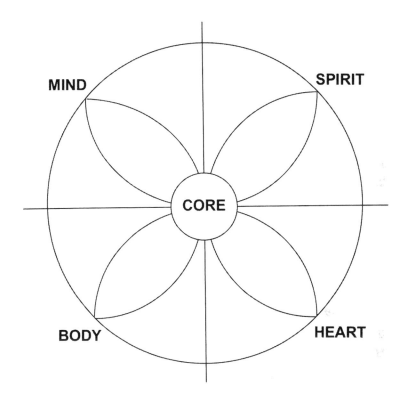

Human Nature Compass

The Human Nature Compass gives you the ability to discern a counselee's moment-to-moment functioning. If the counselee has a dead zone (a decommissioned component of human nature), or overly exaggerates another component (perhaps by thinking at the expense of feeling), you will notice this and start finding ways to help them discover their whole human nature, in itself a therapeutic thing to do. By engaging a counselee's Human Nature Compass, you utilize a "multilevel framework" that enjoys a high correlation with actualizing growth (Allport, 1937; Millon at al., 2004; Lazarus, 2006; Corey, 2009; Montgomery, 2008).

If one of your sessions overly focuses on emotional catharsis, you will know to spend a portion of the next session on cognitive integration, since emotional release without cognitive meaning has little staying power in overall learning. If your counselee has repressed bodily awareness so as to be oblivious to muscle tension or shallow breathing, you'll help them relax the body in order to live through it with greater zest. Or if your counselee has little or no prayer life, you will support their spiritual growth by encouraging open-ended conversations with Christ and greater visceral trust in the Holy Spirit.

Compass Therapy seeks to make normative a holistic understanding of human nature that intersects the fields of pastoral counseling, pastoral ministry, applied theology, the psychology of religion, spiritual direction, pastoral psychotherapy, and compass psychotheology.

Now for a closer look at the four dimensions of human nature. Then in the next four chapters I will apply them to actual sessions.

Mind

Thinking is a cognitive event that occurs in the frontal lobe of the cerebral cortex. Persons can think thoughts with or without emotion or movement. In 1902 Auguste Rodin created a sculpture titled, "The Thinker." By reading the body language, you can tell that the man is pensively meditating about some inner struggle.

This is how counselees look when they are inwardly absorbed, trying to sort out what to tell you. They're not sure what is relevant to the current problem and what isn't. That is why Freud developed the psychoanalytic dictum, "Say everything that comes into your mind, without censoring anything." Beyond struggling to know what to disclose, counselees usually want to keep up a good front to convince us that they are, after all, good and capable human beings, despite their needs and vulnerabilities.

The pastoral counselor's mind is also at work, in the form of providing new knowledge, suggesting interpretations for the counselee's consideration, offering perspective on a problem, and developing periodic summaries that state what has been covered and what lies ahead.

Additionally, your counselee is thinking between sessions about how to apply new insights toward the solving of current problems. How well counselees can analytically reflect on their therapeutic experience defines the quality of their participation, and may well be the single most influential factor for a positive outcome in counseling (Orlinsky, Grawe & Parks, 1994).

Heart

Feelings reflect arousal of the limbic system deep inside the brain. Feelings possess psychological, physiological, and even spiritual dimensions. Part of effective counseling is helping people recognize when they are having a feeling, and learn to label it accurately.

Some perennial emotions that may need sorting out include the range between feeling joyful and sad, hopeful and despairing, elated and depressed, loving and angry, excited and numb, secure and anxious, confident and guilty, trusting and jealous, appreciative and resentful, serene and frustrated, interested and bored, intrigued and repulsed, ecstatic and agonized, proud and ashamed, reassured and terrified, or caring and indifferent.

E-motions represent physiological energy that is "in motion." Emotions express the energy of personality and are always changing, like the flow of water in a river. It is when some inner conflict has dammed up the flow of feelings like a beaver dam that persons become mired in anxiety or depression. This accounts for the unconscious pressure that floods out in cathartic expression when the beaver dam is therapeutically removed.

In order to develop a healthy personality and fulfilling relationships, all counselees need practice not only in identifying their feelings, but also in thinking about them constructively, and expressing them diplomatically to others and to God.

Body

The field of physiological psychology reveals that there are two different nervous systems in every person. The first is the central nervous system (CNS), which allows a person to stand up and walk, drink a glass of water, or open and close a door. The central nervous system connects skeleton with muscle, and is innervated through the sensorimotor band across the top of the cerebral cortex.

The second nervous system, though less conspicuous, is by far the most important one in counseling. This is the autonomic or "automatic" nervous system (ANS) where respiration, circulation, digestion, elimination, and systemic regulation occur, as well as the daily maintenance of every cell in the body. The ANS can be influenced in dramatic ways. For instance, a professor walks into her class and announces that she's giving a surprise pop quiz that will account for one-fifth of the semester grade. Within microseconds, blood pressure shoots up, pulses quicken, hands clench, and a few students practically stop breathing.

It works the same in counseling, only you can use the ANS for beneficial results. With a few well-chosen words, or even a purposeful shift in your body language, you can easily influence your counselee's attitude and bodily state. This week when a counselee starts manifesting anxiety, try relaxing your own body by letting your voice have resonance and breathing from your diaphragm, slowly and easily. Do you remember earlier when I mentioned letting your hands melt into your lap? Add this gesture, too. And watch how, before long, your counselee begins to relax, since you are giving such strong environmental signals that everything is okay. What is happening is that the direct communication of your "at-ease" body language becomes an unconscious suggestion that your counselee's ANS translates into a physiological relaxation response.

This "stay and play" mode of the autonomic nervous system is the opposite of the "fight or flight" mode that the slightest hint of threat can trigger. So especially when you are offering a novel interpretation of a counselee's behavior for consideration, or when you are exploring an emotionally-charged past memory, you'll want to do so in a warm and relaxing way.

Spirit

When working with non-religious counselees, or counselees who adhere to the teaching of various world religions, human spirituality can be thought of as the realm of values, meaning, and ultimate concern that promotes serenity and truth.

Adherents of Christianity, Judaism, Islam, Hinduism, Buddhism, Taoism, Confucianism, the New Age movement, and agnosticism reveal significant differentiation in their perception of spirituality. Nevertheless, a common theme often echoes Christ's teaching to love God with your whole being and love your neighbor as yourself.

Or, if the person doesn't believe in a theistic conception of God, surrendering to a Higher Power is valuable in order to find meaning beyond the autonomous self.

And if a Higher Power is excluded from religious belief, then there is usually a quest for truth in terms of freedom from illusions and commitment to social justice.

Whatever the spiritual orientation of the counselee, the pastoral counselor can personally draw upon the unique message of Christian faith and doctrine that God is a loving Trinity, providing a platform for therapeutic helping that spiritually interfaces with Christ as mediator between God and persons, the Holy Spirit as Advocate or "One called alongside to help," and God the Father Almighty, who together form the ontological foundation of human nature and hold the key to its fulfillment. For an in-depth exploration of this theme, I refer you to *Trusting in the Trinity: Compass Psychotheology Applied* (Montgomery & Montgomery, 2009).

The work of pastoral counseling, then, shares elements of reconciling people to themselves, others, and God; imparting skill-sets for living effectively, blessing them with good will and compassionate understanding. This therapeutic healing stimulates spiritual growth in counselees, in rhythm with cognitive clarification, emotional modulation, and physical relaxation.

6. Mending the Mind

In this and the next three chapters I want to highlight how you can engage a particular aspect of human nature in order to reach that dimension of your counselee's being, and in so doing, help the counselee find healing in that area and consequently develop a more holistic human nature.

Let's focus on how to engage, heal, and integrate the mind, with its valuable assets of analyzing data, storing what is learned, and estimating probable consequences of certain decisions.

Most people use their minds without thinking about the mind they are using. They have thoughts without examining these thoughts. They live out beliefs and expectations that were programmed into their psyche somewhere along life's way, but have not updated these mental assumptions to their current circumstances or the evolving goals that new life challenges bring.

A thirty-year-old man reveals to you that he had three major goals when he was twenty: work hard and make money; have fun letting off steam with the boys at the local bar; and get married.

By the second session, precisely because you've been concentrating on his story and looking for how he has engaged his mind in lifespan development, you realize that he did indeed achieve all three original goals, but because he never integrated them with new information concerning how to love and care for his wife, she has ended up alone in the marriage for ten years, and that is why she's left him.

You present this as a tentative hypothesis, something you are modeling for him to learn to do, in this fashion:

"Bob, from what you shared, it sounds like your company thinks you're the best worker they've got, and your buddies have a ball with you when you all get hammered. Now I know you are absolutely heartbroken that Tanya has left you, and you want to do anything possible to get her back. But it seems to me that without revising your assumptions about life and really changing your thinking about marriage, even if she came back on a Friday she'd be gone again on Monday."

"I guess you just pretty much hit the nail on the head. I was raised with five older sisters and a mom who doted on me. I guess I never learned to pay attention to anybody's needs but mine."

"I think that's part of it, Bob. But here's the fascinating thing. You're only boring when you're at home with Tanya. The rest of the time people think you're a livewire who can be totally depended upon to come through with what they need."

"That's true enough. Everybody but Tanya thinks I'm a great guy."

"Well, I have a suggestion for you. I believe you have it in you to take that same emotional gusto, friendly smile, and sincere loyalty that you've been giving your guy pals all these years and transfer a portion of it Tanya's way. You know, like taking funds out of one account that has abundant cash and depositing them in another account that's overdrawn. If you can just remember to keep doing that, then the emotional satisfaction level of both accounts will do fine. Now, how would you put this in your own words?"

(In this way, you've introduced Bob to a new theory of why his marriage has failed, a new way to understand how his past is connected to his present and future, and an innovative idea for making new decisions that can develop more satisfying outcomes. But it is very important after a mental exchange like this, especially when the stakes are so high, that you create room for Bob to find his own way of construing the information, developing his own cognitive-linguistic pathways for expressing these insights, thereby converting them from short-term intuitions to permanent memory).

"Well, I guess it's that I didn't want to get over being a spoiled kid when I became an adult. And I did know how to work and play. So when my friends started getting married, I figured I'd do that too. It never occurred to me that I needed to make changes in my thinking."

"That's an excellent analysis of the problem. Now how do you see the solution?"

"I think the main problem is that I always thought women came from outer space, that they had their own needs that didn't make any sense to me. But from what you're saying, Tanya may be a lot like my buddies, and that if I can learn to treat her with the same respect and attention I give them, she'll find out I'm not so bad after all."

"I believe you've developed a solid plan here, Bob. I know it's not going to be easy, but I want you to keep thinking like this, and trying out some new attitudes and behaviors toward Tanya, without expecting her to change her mind overnight. Let's work together to keep you on track until treating her with love and sensitivity becomes your new track record in this relationship. May I say a prayer of blessing to close the session?"

"Please do."

In this example you utilized pastoral counseling to reveal informational deficiencies in the counselee's mind, and to supply updated principles that the counselee translated into his own mental framework, principles that forge links in developmental growth that will not only mend his mind, but also bring more of his whole human nature to the relationship with his estranged wife.

The Compass Therapy approach to pastoral counseling specializes in integrating polar opposites, transforming them into rhythmic wholes. This brings up a paradox in pastoral counseling: you pass judgment while also expressing empathy; you analyze your counselee's mental functioning, including scrutinizing the content of ideas, beliefs, and expectations, while at the same time maintaining emotional rapport; and above all, you keep an open mind while having your own values.

The Counselor's Open Mind

The first thing you want to establish with your counselees is their freedom to say anything without evoking your distress, disapproval, or displeasure. Pastoral counseling that is too moralistic or caught up in applying scriptural mandates for counselee behavior can break down at this point. Counselees quickly perceive that they are not free to share their raw mental experiences because the counselor turns these into opportunities to pontificate. They learn to conceal information, deceive the counselor, and leave counseling as soon as possible in order to be done with the ordeal of feeling cross-examined and found morally deficient.

In Compass Therapy you learn to consider anything human as worthy of understanding. And you learn to distance yourself emotionally and morally from what the counselee is disclosing, so that your face, eyes, and body language do not convey shock or negative judgment.

In training graduate students in counseling, I often set up dyads for role-playing a counseling session, giving secret instructions to "counselees" to disclose intense presenting problems, such as having a marital affair, masturbating compulsively, talking about an incest experience, or using crib notes to pass exams for a Master's degree in counseling!

56

The aim is to help those who are role-playing counselors to hear with equanimity any human experience, and to keep the conversation going by showing an open mind to the counselee's point of view.

Having an open mind doesn't mean that you agree with the person, that you have no values, or that you aren't guiding them in directions that lead toward health and away from dysfunction. It just means they can talk openly to you without censoring themselves, and trust the values you bring forth precisely because you understand and accept where they are coming from.

The beauty of an open mind allows you to begin praying with them using their own vivid description of difficulties, which helps them grasp that God, too, is open-minded, that God, too, is listening with curiosity and warm concern, and is worthy of their consideration as "the Great Companion" (William James, 1902).

The Power of Ideas and Concepts

Compass Therapy suggests that counseling not follow a pattern where the pastoral counselor sits and waits for the counselee to speak. This passive style of counseling was originally developed by Carl Rogers in the 1950s, and called Client-centered Therapy. This required waiting for the client's self-motivation in expressing ideas or feelings, followed by restating what the counselee said in fresh words, including the emotional nuances that the counselee seemed to be experiencing.

There is wisdom in this approach when it is utilized primarily to keep emotional rapport with a counselee, but when it dominates the whole counseling process, the counselee's mind is not challenged with new ideas, suggestions for growth and change, or conceptual models that the counselee can start using. In a personal conversation with Rogers toward the end of his career, I asked if he might adjust his method in light of all that he had learned. He said,

"Dan, I believe my method would really benefit by the counselor becoming more active than I had originally supposed. I now believe that engaging the client with ideas would provide a good balance with my emphasis on reflecting a client's feelings."

Compass Therapy incorporates Roger's astute assessment by encouraging in every session a regular rhythm between reflecting emotions and expanding ideas, between following the energy of counselee motivation while actively shaping the dialogue toward concepts that clarify confusion. For instance, showing counselees the Human Nature Compass and exploring how it pertains to them provides a memorable tool for self-awareness that they carry into the future.

Or take the example of a young woman in her mid-twenties who is disturbed about her pattern of succumbing to intercourse with dates who put sexual pressure on her. She shares her chagrin in discovering that this casual sex leaves her stranded by a succession of men who use her for gratification and move on.

From a Compass Therapy perspective, she needs to cathart her frustration and confusion without feeling negatively judged, but also to receive a gradual education about the risks of AIDS and herpes, the phenomenon of how sexual promiscuity short-circuits communication and communion, and if appropriate, an explanation as to why Scripture opposes sex outside of marriage in order to preserve people from the fragmenting outcome of orgasm without spiritual and psychological intimacy. Once these concepts have gestated, and the woman has new cognitive clarity with which to resist narcissistic seductions, she is able to say "no" to sexual advances while standing up for a relationship that offers more mental, emotional, sensual, and spiritual maturity. Now she can apply the Human Nature Compass and other conceptual ideas to her quest for a meaningful and lasting man/woman bond.

Bibliotherapy

I recommend suggesting an appropriate book at the outset of counseling to build a counselee's motivation by immediately engaging the mind. I often use *The Self Compass: Charting Your Personality In Christ*, because it helps counselees discover how personality patterns perpetuate many difficulties, while at the same time motivating them to participate in psychological and spiritual growth.

I'm sure you have your own favorite book.

Keep in mind that reading a therapeutically effective book while in counseling accomplishes several purposes: 1) It involves counselees in thinking constructively about their issues in ways that make it easier to express; 2) It lightens the burden of counseling by eliciting their direct involvement early on; 3) It introduces ideas that help them carry over what happens in counseling to daily life; and 4) Reading about how other people grow and change moves them away from merely reciting problems into creative problem solving.

I like when a counselee comes into a second or third session with a highlighted book and says, "I think I've got a lot in common with the Worrier pattern (or Pleaser, Storyteller, Loner, Arguer, Rule-breaker, Boaster or Controller)," or, "I'm really relieved that the Self Compass makes sense out of my temper problems," or best of all, "I really want to become an individual in Christ."

Framing Counselees As Heroes of Their Life Narrative

Human beings have an existential need for visibility; that is, recognition and validation that they are special and their lives matter. When counselees feel stuck in problems they can't find their way through, it takes a toll on self-esteem. Compass Therapy seeks to strengthen their self-image, promoting redemptive hope by viewing them as uniquely heroic in their efforts to overcome difficulty.

Miguel was seeing me for help in solving a relationship problem. He had been dating the same woman for five years, yet she was still holding him at arms length whenever he mentioned marriage. In the first two sessions I had learned that Miguel had experienced a fairly tempestuous adolescence, including a good amount of fighting, cussing, and delinquency. He and Monica attended the same church, but this didn't stop his old behaviors from sabotaging his efforts at emotional intimacy.

Now in the third session, Miguel says, "I just don't get it. Monica knows I love her. Why won't she marry me?"

"I wonder if it has something to do with the way you respond to her in conversations?"

"Well, she does say that I cut her off and don't understand her feelings. But it's boring when she gets emotionally worked up. I really don't want to hear about it."

"So from your view, it's like she's always asking for more emotion than you're willing to give, and you get sick of her carping."

(This is an emotional reflection, designed to make sure Miguel feels that I empathize with his frustration, before expanding his thought to help mend his mind).

"Exactly. She drives me crazy that way!"

"I think I have a hypothesis about what's going on. Would you like to hear it?"

(I'm now signaling to Miguel that we are changing to another part of his human nature—his mind—and I'm doing so respectfully by asking his permission).

"Sure."

"Well, from what you told me in our first session about the pretty aggressive crowd you grew up with, and from your identifying with the Arguer and Boaster personality patterns when you read the Self Compass book, I think we can say that you might be showing hostility and rudeness to her a lot more than you've realized."

Miguel laughs. "She'd agree with that. But verbal sparring comes naturally to me. That's how I make my living in sales. I always have an answer before someone asks the question, and I totally control the conversation. Isn't that a good thing?"

"It's a communication style that may work in business, but not if your goal is man/woman love."

"Why?"

"How about putting on your thinking cap and telling me?"

Miguel offers a sheepish grin. "Because I don't pay attention to what she's saying?"

"And even more significantly, perhaps because you're not emotionally connected to her while she's speaking."

Miguel sits back and sighs. "But I pride myself on being a good communicator. All my friends say I can talk my way out of anything."

"I think this is the crux of the difficulty. In that fast crowd you grew up around, was it considered a strength to outsmart people with comebacks and put-downs?"

"Yeah. I always came out on top, too."

(Now I administer more truth serum, knowing that if he receives it, I can move toward framing him as a hero of his life's narrative).

"So as long as the conversations were focused on verbal sparring and had a competitive edge, you were the best of the best. But when you developed a man/woman relationship headed for marriage, everything stalled. Is that right?"

Miguel takes another deep breath, his eyes glazing over in thought. "I never thought of it like that before. I've always thought this whole problem was Monica's fault for not being tough enough to handle how I talk to her."

"I wonder if you're on the verge of seeing that perhaps your aggressive speech has inflicted her with a lot of emotional wounds; that maybe she's tried to tell you this but you turned a deaf ear."

Miguel tears up. "She's used that exact word—wounded. I never knew what she meant."

"What are you feeling right now?"

Miguel wipes away a tear. "I feel sorry for being hard on her. Sorry, too, for never understanding her."

(I wait for a few moments as he stares into space, sensing that his mind is assimilating a new theory about his past behavior, and perhaps finding fresh resolve to make attitudinal changes).

"I'm experiencing admiration for you, Miguel, because many individuals who have dished out harsh treatment to a partner aren't willing to acknowledge it. But here you're not only admitting your aggressive communication style, but also feeling empathy for how it's impacted Monica."

"I love her, Dr. Dan. I really do." (His voice quavers with the emotion behind his declaration).

"I feel the sincerity of your love. But it seems like your aggression has the potential to destroy that love, at least on Monica's part. Would you give me permission to point out when I observe traces of this aggressive trend in sessions, so you can become more aware of it?"

"Absolutely. It's so second nature I don't know how to change it. But I don't want to hurt Monica any more."

"Because?"

"Because I want her to love and trust me."

(I want to deepen the cognitive memory trace of his statement and all it conveys).

"Please say this again, even firmer."

His eyes tear slightly once more. "I want Monica to trust me because I start listening to her feelings."

(Now I can place a new frame around Miguel's life narrative, a frame that encompasses the growth he seeks).

"So may we describe you as a man who has finally come to face his combative ways? Who wants to transform his history as a tough-talking teenager into an adult capable of love and respect for the woman he hopes to marry?"

"That's exactly right."

"How would you say this to Monica?

"I guess I would say, 'Hey Babe, I'm really sorry for bad-mouthing you so much. I know it's not right. I want to treat you a lot better."

"That's a solid beginning, Miguel. That's how an aggressive guy can become a hero of love."

It is fun to relax enough in your counseling and coaching practice so that your mind can play with piecing together people's stories, coming up with plausible hypotheses, creating thought experiments they can engage in, and enjoying conversations that creatively explore what's wrong and how to help fix it.

But aren't words like "fun," "relaxing," "playing," "enjoying," and "creative," antithetical to the serious work of counseling? Not really, because it's very worthwhile to build a warm human bond where curiosity and fascination enliven the counseling process, inviting counselees to join in the adventure of human growth.

7. HEALING THE HEART

Working constructively with emotions is crucial to success in pastoral counseling because feelings are the energy of personality. They are literally like an artist's color palette, from which the artist loads his brush to give life, hue, and nuance to a painting. If the artist keeps rinsing the brush between applications, the color will remain vivid and true. But if the artist doesn't regularly clean the brush, paint from former brush strokes will accrue and turn the new applications muddy and dark.

So it is with feelings. During the course of counseling, from first to last session, you are seeking to offer the counselee ways to experience and express emotions that contribute to healthy living, and keep the heart cleansed from clogged-up feelings that would otherwise contaminate the canvas of perception.

What is the nature of clogged-up emotions? I mentioned earlier that human emotions are meant to flow through the body much like water down a river. Sometimes there is a lot of emotion and sometimes there is only a trickle, but what's important here is that emotions are transitory psychophysiological events involving the mid-brain and lower brain stem, but not the neocortex. In a word, emotions feel but don't think. They reflect the more instinctual, subjective part of perception, the gut reaction to what's going on between the environment and the organism in the here and now.

What, then, is the purpose of a feeling? The purpose is to discriminate between liking and disliking, needing and not needing, wanting and not wanting, coping and not coping. Feelings tell people about their own spontaneous interests, preferences, needs, and desires. Once a feeling has served its purpose, it recedes into the background of awareness.

Compass Therapy utilizes the catchall word "Heart" to point toward those inner states that most people experience as emanating from the area of the heart, stomach, and bowels. The Old Testament is especially replete with anthropomorphic references to internal body organs that offer metaphors for how both God and people experience emotion.

Counselees understand immediately when you talk about matters of the heart. When you ask what a counselee is feeling, the person understands that you are inquiring about the most subjective, emotionally colored, and private part of their perception, a part oftentimes so private they can't find words to express it or even know they are feeling it.

Now here's the secret of facilitating the awareness and discrimination of emotions in counselees. Don't judge them! Remember that feelings are transitory physiological processes that need recognition and integration into the personality, not repression and exile to the unconscious.

Thus when a six-year-old boy says he feels like killing his older sister when she twists his wrist, he is experiencing anger and trying to express it so that the feeling will pass through him and dissipate. You don't forbid him to ever speak this way again, but rather seek to expand his metaphors until he comes up with a more diplomatic expression of anger.

Your purpose entails expanding inner emotional states, so that counselees can become more comfortable with emotions in general, and more interested in understanding and defining them. Feeling and thinking can interact rhythmically here, the feeling providing the raw material of direct experience, the thinking providing an analysis of explanatory causes and effects that pertain to the feeling. By repeatedly helping counselees to slow down their communication enough to feel an emotion cleanly, label it accurately, and consider how best to express it, you are helping them come alive.

This principle is so important that if you primarily listen to people's feelings and help to clarify and transform them into meaningful expressions, you will heal a good many people. This is the brilliance of Carl Rogers' historic contribution to counseling theory. I remember him telling me that feelings were the hardest things to put into words because they capture the innermost heart of a person's moment-to-moment experiencing, and because people feel vulnerable when disclosing their deepest feelings.

Modulating Feelings — The Core of Counseling

When it comes to feelings, there are three types of counselees you'll likely meet. The more cognitive and emotionally guarded person holds back feelings, like a squirrel stuffing its pouches with acorns. The opposite occurs with the histrionic counselee who wears the heart on the sleeve, blurting out so many feelings that you can hardly keep up with them. Persons who have already struck a healthy balance between thinking and feeling will use your help to clarify emotions, but then articulate them in their own words.

Here's a key principle in applying Compass Therapy to pastoral counseling: keep it simple. Follow the psychology of the obvious. Help counselees name, understand, and utilize their emotions so that they are well served by them.

For the cognitive-oriented counselee, you place less emphasis on an exchange of ideas or verbal discussions that bypass personal feelings. This counselee will at first tend to defend against displaying emotion through a mechanism called intellectualization. What you want to do is slow down the process of this person's communication so that the inner palette of emotional nuance is discovered and gradually actualized.

You can say at some point: "You know, it strikes me that some of the deeper things inside you hold clues about what you really want and need. Might I have your permission now and then to reflect what seems like a feeling, to bring into our dialogue some of the emotional undertones of what you're saying?"

Or, to someone who masks the flow of inner emotion through the habitual use of indiscriminate phrases like, "I feel weird," "It doesn't really matter," and "That doesn't really bother me," you might say, "How about we try to flesh out more clearly some of what's going on inside you, so that you can use these inner feelings as part of your decision-making process?"

You don't need to overdo this by stereotypically asking, "How do you feel about that?" It's more that, among other things, you know the value of raising the counselee's emotional IQ, encouraging them to trust, discern, and integrate the emotions they experience.

For counselees who ooze feelings but are not in the habit of examining and sorting them out, you take the opposite tack. You intervene in the cascading waves of emotion by asking thoughtful questions or making summary statements. You literally play the role of a cognitive neocortex for them until they learn to think about their own feelings.

A man strings together a flood of negative feelings about his ex-wife. You summarize: "So from your view, Ellen had nothing going for her except her constant demands for emotional intimacy from you." This in itself is provocative, for it causes the man to shift into a cognitive mindset from which he says, "Well, it's not like she didn't contribute anything.

She did raise our three kids because I was traveling so much. And she took care of the monthly budget, since that isn't my forte." Now you've got him integrating thinking and feeling, and though it may take some doing before he can cultivate this new habit, at least he is gaining experience in slowing down his emotional flow enough to think about what he is experiencing.

To another such counselee you periodically say things like: "Let's slow down a moment and see which one of your feelings is the most important right now." "Can you elaborate on that for a moment?" Or, "What is your theory about why you always get so mad when you are dealing with a salesperson?"

By helping your counselees learn how to understand and modulate their feelings, you are giving them the versatility a pianist shows when integrating the loud, soft, and mute pedals in playing a piece of music.

The Meaning of Repression

In the larger scope of counseling, you are working with individuals who are sometimes *re*pressing, sometimes *sup*pressing, and sometimes *ex*pressing their emotions. By creating a warm interpersonal climate that is conducive to emotional exploration and discovery, you help counselees learn to sense and manage their feelings in personal and interpersonal ways.

Freud discovered the defense mechanism of repression, which occurs when a person feels temporarily overwhelmed by a powerful emotion. It takes a considerable expenditure of physiological energy to push an emotion out of awareness and keep it from re-emerging. This drastic measure is accomplished through a series of instantaneous maneuvers. The repressed emotion is disowned so that it takes the appearance of something foreign and threatening, not something that belongs to the person. The person blocks it from cognitive assimilation by locking it in the dungeon of muscle tension, which entails tensing the interlocking actin and myocin protein molecules in millions of muscle fibers that extend throughout the body, forming bands of muscular armor that keep the emotion buried and inaccessible, a kind of iron curtain that bars the emotion from consciousness. This is why counselees are "in the dark" about feelings they have repressed, and it is why these feelings cannot be brought into the light of awareness without a temporary sense of anxiety and foreboding.

However, good counseling makes the unconscious conscious by creating an interpersonal atmosphere of trust and acceptance, releasing previously bound up energy and repressed emotion into spontaneous catharsis. For this reason, you don't need to feel alarmed if your counselee experiences a few minutes of crying, wringing the hands, or grimacing. Rather, you coach them as gently as possible into a Lamaze-like birth of emotion by saying, "This is very good that you're in touch with this feeling...Breathe and let it flow ...It's safe here...That's good, stay in touch with this emotion while it flows through your body...It's okay to have this feeling, it can't hurt you now...Relax and give this emotion a new voice. You're taking this feeling out of the dark and bringing it into our presence, where we can finally understand what it's been trying to say."

You can see as the person responds to your coaching how the feeling is un-repressed before your eyes, because it will grow more vivid and intense only to a certain point, but when the muscular and psychological resistance melts enough to allow the counselee to surrender fully to the feeling, it quickly passes through the body and is integrated into the whole of their human nature. Then lo and behold, it dissipates to the point where it no longer bothers them. This is called "expanding the affect" and "normalizing a feeling."

Immediately following an emotional catharsis, you soothe a person's temporary loss of control by saying, "That was excellent emotional expression." Often they will smile with pride, a kind of self-congratulation for the courage they expressed to stay in touch with the emotion long enough for it to pass, like a kidney stone, through their system. Next you move into debriefing, which means talking over the original situation that led to the repressed emotion, and exploring healthy ways to handle similar situations in the counselee's current life. You might say, "What have you just learned from this powerful emotion?" Or, "Now that you've brought this old memory into awareness, what do you think about it?"

By now your counselee will tap into your relaxed curiosity and articulate their own creative insights.

Some particularly traumatic events in a counselee's history may need several passes in order to fully assimilate and work through, as when there exists considerable bitterness in divorce after twenty years of marriage, or when sexual abuse or rape is involved. The healing can take place over the course of several months, but eventually the trapped emotions of rage, terror, or grief pass through the self system so that the spiritual core—not the repressed emotions—can take its rightful place as the center of the self. Other emotions, however, can be assimilated almost immediately and not present any further problems.

The Rhythm Between Suppression and Expression

The constant shift between expressing and restraining emotions that goes on in normal social discourse is like the rhythm between the accelerator and brakes in driving a car across town. People need both functions in complementary interplay all the time in order to safely arrive where they are heading.

Through modeling and coaching about how to diplomatically communicate feelings to others, you help counselees mature in personality and relationships. You help them become more open about recognizing when they are having an emotion, and then thinking about the context of the feeling: "What is stirring up this feeling? Am I reacting to something in the present or reactivating a memory from the past? Do I need to alter my thinking in order to change the feeling? Do I need to express the feeling or simply be aware that I'm experiencing it?"

There is real wisdom attached to the notion of counting to ten before expressing a strong feeling. This ability to "sit on a feeling" long enough to reflect on it, prior to conveying it to others, is called emotional suppression. You educate your counselees that while emotional repression is unproductive, emotional suppression is a perfectly healthy adult relational skill that assists them to overlook or diminish feelings that would be disruptive or even harmful if expressed, and by the same token, leads them to intentionally express any emotion that contributes to their wellbeing or helps another person to understand them better. There is room for expressing hurt, disagreement, or even anger, but only after enough reflection has transpired that they can do so diplomatically.

Likewise, counselees need encouragement and sometimes modeling to know how to express praise, compliments, enjoyment, and excitement without getting so carried away with these positive feelings that they become histrionic. Even feelings like love often need a little coaching so that the counselee expresses caring without becoming invasive or presumptuous with another person.

One caveat about working with feelings lies in giving up the need to make a counselee happy, whether at the end of each session, or as a consequence of the course of counseling. Some individuals create such conflicted circumstances that happiness will elude them for many years, while others cling to rigid personality patterns that perpetuate misery.

Here we must surrender any vestiges we have of a "Messiah Complex." We can't heal all people all the time, but we can accept the reality that we do the best we can, stopping short of taking responsibility for a person's life and choices—even God doesn't do that! Yet most sessions can end with a pleasant emotional tone, in that the pastoral/therapeutic bond creates a fellowship that does indeed bring comfort.

8. Benefiting The Body

Most people assume that counseling involves talking things over to work through problems and discover new solutions. But this is too narrow a perspective. An effective pastoral counselor watches body language and knows a good deal about the body. The Hebrew notion that a human person incorporates the mind-heart-body-spirit as a holistic being created in the image of God captures the body's importance.

So when you first greet a counselee, I recommend a warm handshake and a strong greeting. "Hi Mary Lou." "Welcome, Javier." You are sending visual, auditory, and sensory energy from your body into the counselee's body, and the counselee's "self" suddenly feels welcomed, the result of millions of neurons firing throughout the organism, creating a perception that your office is a good place to be.

This psycho-sensory-spiritual rapport is the glue that holds counseling together, helping counselees to face hard facts and experience difficult feelings, knowing that you are right there with them in a tangible way.

We receive a glimpse of this in Jesus, the Son of Man who comes among us to share our burdens and lighten our load. Jesus enjoys eating and drinking with regular people, much to the consternation of the scrupulously religious folks, and he uses his body often in communication and for psychological, spiritual, and physical healing. Picture him writing with his fingertip in the dirt when he rescues the woman caught in adultery from an angry crowd, or mixing his saliva with dirt to apply to a blind man's eyes, or hugging little children.

God knows that people need visceral involvement in their lives and relationships—freedom to let the body play a natural role in communication and communion. But when stress builds up and tightens the muscles of the face, neck, back, stomach, and chest, the body stiffens, becoming more like a sarcophagus than a living presence.

Knowing this, you train yourself to observe your counselee's whole body during sessions. Here is a list of significant bodily events that convey vital information:

1) The eyes tend to reveal a person's real feelings. You want to gaze gently at a counselee's eyes, without ever staring. Sometimes I purposely break off my gaze by looking down at the floor or off to the side, especially if the counselee is pausing for thought. This helps the counselee not feel under scrutiny, as though under a microscope. Self-consciousness interrupts their train of thought and causes them to pull back and even artificially alter their communication.

You want instead for counselees to feel so caught up in disclosing what is important for them that they don't even think about it. So watching them in a gentle way promotes this effect and encourages their feelings to flow through their eyes. Especially notice the microsecond or two when their eyes tear slightly, because this signals that they are in contact with emotionally significant material, cueing you to expand what they are talking about into fuller expression.

2) God has designed some forty-six facial muscles that allow for the widest range of expression imagi-

nable. Think for a moment how the face looks when a person experiences fear, anxiety, depression, curiosity, awe, love, hate, revenge, bitterness, or terror. You can help counselees relax their facial muscles by letting your own face become expressive in the counseling dialogue.

I realize that certain schools of counseling discourage counselors from showing emotion, but I disagree, perhaps because my model for doing therapy is Jesus. Letting your face show sorrow when your counselee experiences grief honors your counselee while revealing your empathy. Letting your face light up with joy when the counselee shares good news or makes an exciting therapeutic discovery confirms to the counselee that you share their delight. Letting your face show curiosity or fascination when they are trying to find the right words to capture how something happened or what they felt as it occurred, conveys to them that you are interested, that you care.

The only two facial expressions that are counterproductive in counseling are anger and boredom. This is where therapeutic discipline comes to your aid, knowing that you are in session with counselees for their sake and not yours, for their wellbeing and not for your comfort. So any feelings of exasperation, irritability, or impatience that you feel must be covered up in the sense that you stay one step removed from the feeling until you can reflect upon it after the session.

3) The chest and abdomen are extremely important to observe during sessions, and once you train yourself in such observation, you will regularly notice fluctuations in breathing that are therapeutically significant. Since stress makes people hypervigilant and tense, counselees under stress breathe shallowly

through the thorax, or upper part of the chest, rather than deeply through the abdomen.

Shallow breathing takes extreme form in the hyperventilation of a panic attack. What actually happens is that the person becomes fearful and starts holding their breath. This starves the brain of oxygenated blood, creating dizziness and a shrinking perceptual field that focuses exclusively on the feeling of being threatened. The body reacts by further tightening the chest and stomach, constricting the breathing even more. Finally, a person is left panting for air and panic takes over. The brain can't think and the body can't relax, and it all starts with shallow breathing as a response to fear.

The reverse of panic and dread is the deep abdominal breathing that many women learn as a prerequisite to natural childbirth. Knowing this physical principle lets you encourage all of your counselees to breathe more deeply when they are sharing memories or experiences that make them tense.

The truth is that anxiety and relaxation cannot co-exist in the same physical space, and since abdominal breathing promotes peace and serenity along with general physical relaxation, it can become a part of the counselee's lifestyle that reduces stress by increasing visceral wellbeing. So when I observe constricted breathing, I say, "Go ahead and relax your breathing for a moment, and then continue what you are saying," or, "Take a couple of deep breaths to melt this tension in your body."

4) Just like the first violin sets the tone for an orchestra, the voice is the first violin of pastoral counseling. You can train yourself to hear the smallest vacillation in the counselee's voice, and to help them relax enough for a rich resonance to replace histrionic

breathlessness, nondescript monotone, or brusque delivery.

You do this in part through direct modeling; that is, learning how to relax enough during sessions that your voice shows a range of modulation and vocal flexibility that encourages a similar richness of expression in the counselee.

In addition, it is okay to say to the person who speaks so softly that you can barely hear them, "You know, I wonder if you might concentrate on turning up the volume of your voice so that you can hear your own feelings better, and so that other people can feel connected to you." Or to the person who speaks loudly all the time, "I wonder if you are aware that your voice is so forceful that many of your more sensitive feelings are glossed over."

Beyond feedback aimed at strengthening a person's awareness of how they are communicating, you listen for nuances of emotion that appear in vocalization from time to time, but which your counselee might miss if you didn't stop to amplify the feeling.

Both fear and anger add a tremulous tone to the vocal chords, yet are entirely different emotions. Also, the intensity that comes when a person is in direct contact with emotionally significant material, like a feeling of sadness, longing, or animosity, manifests itself in the tenor of the voice, once you learn to recognize it. Knowing this helps you clarify their feelings.

Direct Body Techniques

Aside from observing a counselee's ongoing bodily expressions during pastoral counseling, there are direct ways of working with the body that benefit people.

The two body techniques I use most involve *belly breathing* and *differential relaxation*. You preface each one with an explanation of why you are initiating the technique and how it will impart a beneficial life skill.

For the breathing technique I say something like, "Theresa, one of the best ways to reduce stress and increase your ability to relax and think involves deepening your breathing. With your permission I'd like to take five minutes and teach you this skill."

"Will this help me feel less nervous around people?"

"Yes, it will. Now just fold your hands in your lap like I am doing, and take a deep breath, as deep as you can, and hold it for a few moments." She does so, watching how I simultaneously model the exercise. "Very good. Now let all the air out slowly, like deflating a balloon. Keep pushing the air out until it is all gone." She does so. "Now take another deep breath, slowly filling your lower lungs with air in the abdominal area until they're full." She does so. "Now do this a couple of more times while I explain what's happening. When you push out all the air, you are exhaling carbon dioxide from the lungs and body. Then when you fill your lungs with air by relaxing your belly muscles, you are drawing in a fresh supply of oxygenated blood that feeds your brain and body, providing plenty of energy for thinking clearly and feeling calm. Does this make sense?"

She nods and continues the deep breathing exercise. After about three minutes of doing the exercise, I say, "Now I'd like you to scan your body right now and tell me what you are aware of."

Theresa looks thoughtful, and then says, "I'm feeling kind of heavy in my arms and legs. It's a pleasant feeling. And very relaxing."

"This is what it means to experience bodily serenity, which is the opposite of tension and anxiety. Take one more deep breath and think, 'This is how I feel when I'm deeply relaxed.'"

She does so. I say, "To complete the exercise, imagine yourself at home, at work, or on the freeway, remembering now and then to breathe deeply and relax. This is how you experience serenity throughout the day. Over time, this can become second nature to you."

As simple as this technique seems, it is life changing for persons to learn how to relax at periodic moments throughout the day. Not only do they minimize tension and anxiety, but worry diminishes as well. It becomes easier to laugh, play, pray, and relate to people without building up body tension. With time even the capillaries, veins, and arteries of the circulatory system relax and open up, allowing for a maximum flow of blood into every area of the body for cell maintenance, detoxification of wastes, and energy production. Work, rest, and sleep become easier. Bodily aches and pains, which often reflect chronically tensed muscles, lessen.

Deep breathing can enhance the counselee's ability to sensually enjoy the physiological serenity the Holy Spirit can impart, thus making prayer a more comfortable and renewing experience.

The second technique I often use is called *differential relaxation.* I use this when I notice a chronic pattern of tension in the muscles of the jaw, neck, shoulders, or hands. Again, I always explain why I'm introducing the technique and how the consequences are beneficial.

"Jim, it seems like you carry a lot of tension in your jaw. I think this might be related to the anger you mentioned toward your boss. But it can become a problem in itself because unresolved tension interrupts your ability to relax and sets you on edge like a stretched rubber band that's ready to snap. Can we focus on this for a few moments?"

"Sure. Actually, my dentist has talked about making a mouth guard for me because I grind my teeth so much."

I nod. "So our technique will contribute to the solution. Now what I'd like you to do is clench your teeth on purpose for about thirty seconds. Go ahead." Jim clenches his teeth and I keep talking. "Feel this tension that you're creating in your jaw and mouth area. Become curious about how you can create it and how you can make it go away." I'm introducing a novel concept that what Jim has previously considered an involuntary condition is actually under his control. "Now relax your jaw completely, right to the point where there is a space between your upper and lower palate, so your jaw muscle goes slack."

He does so. "I feel a little silly with my mouth hanging open," he says with a grin.

I slacken my jaw muscle and let my mouth hang open. "Me too! Now tense your jaw muscle for thirty seconds, studying the sensation of muscle contraction that you are creating." He does so. "Now melt those muscles and see what new sensations come."

He does so. "Well, I like it better when my jaw relaxes."

"How come?"

"I don't know, but it's like my whole neck starts relaxing, and that's a real relief."

"Do it once more," I suggest. "And this time notice how the jaw tension spreads to your neck and breathing and whole body." He concentrates on the clench and takes in the new information from his body. "Now melt your jaw muscle, let your upper and lower palette part slightly, and let this relaxation spread to your neck and shoulders." He does so. "What are you discovering?"

"Well, when I squeeze my jaw my whole body tenses up and when I relax it, everything loosens up."

"Excellent observation. So this week I encourage you to experiment further with this tension and relaxation phenomenon at home, at work, and while driving. See if you can make a mind/body connection that lets you feel the jaw tension when it occurs, and melt it away as an act of will like you've been doing here."

Now if I were a pastoral counselor reading this book right now, I might be thinking, "What is my congregation going to think if word gets around that I'm teaching counselees to relax their jaws?" My suggestion, however, is that when body relaxation techniques are part of your counseling armamentarium, and when you use them appropriately to help individuals develop more stress-free, peaceable, and enjoyable lives, the word will get around that you really know your stuff.

9. Inspiring The Spirit

The spirit, the most elusive component of human nature, evokes a host of references in general culture. Athletic teams play with spirit or else lose their spirit. A close companion lifts the spirit of a depressed friend. There is the artistic spirit, the spirit of battle, the spirit of the times, the spirit of truth, the Spirit of God, and the human spirit.

Why shouldn't we, as pastoral counselors and consecrated mental health workers, recognize, nurture, and inspire the spirit of our counselees? The merging of psychology and spirituality provides an understanding of human nature that supports a counselee's pursuit of a meaningful life. Indeed, spirituality is a genuine frontier for research in helping people develop increased wellbeing and fulfillment (Moss, 2002; Miller & Thoreson, 2003; Seeman et al., 2003; Crossley & Salter, 2005; Shaw et al., 2005; Anandarajah, 2008). Thus it is perfectly appropriate for a pastoral counselor to suggest that God is present in counseling, offering redemptive hope that helps remove obstacles blocking the way to wholeness.

In some contexts, a pastoral counselor's freedom to invoke God's blessing through prayer is part of the counseling process. This is especially true in pastoral ministry, spiritual direction, and church-based counseling centers. On the other hand, there are contexts in which it is unwise to mention God in a personal way, such as the name of Christ. I remember at a state-run mental institution where I had been invited to visit patients, a chaplain said to me in the corridor, "Now Dan, you can pray for people in your heart, and you can make generalized references to the Psalms, but please don't dare mention Jesus." I did as he requested so as not to jeopardize his ministry there.

Even so, there is a considerable range of opportunity where spirituality is welcomed covertly, if not overtly, and this may be where a significant number of the new generation of pastoral counselors find themselves.

The Spirit Moves Where The Spirit Wills

As a professor at Pepperdine University Graduate School of Psychology, I found myself in one of these places. Pepperdine is religiously affiliated with the Churches of Christ, reaches out to students of all races and faiths, and pursues academic excellence within a context that celebrates and extends the spiritual and ethical ideals of the Christian faith.

Yet it was made very clear to me by the dean that any form of Christian witness or prayer was not acceptable in the classroom. The fear was that non-Christian or non-religious students would take offense, and besides, Christian faith ought to be lived in one's life, not articulated in the classroom. I understood and accepted this unwritten policy. Nevertheless, some students knew of my relationship to Christ, and perhaps because of that saw me more as a pastoral counselor than a professional psychologist. Greg was such a student.

Following a class one afternoon, Greg called me aside in the hallway and said, "Dan, can we talk privately?"

"Sure," I said. I opened the door to an empty classroom and we sat down in two desks. "What's on your mind?"

"Well," he said, looking suddenly unsure, "I just wanted to get something off my chest and you're the one I've chosen."

"I'm honored. Go ahead."

"My life has fallen to pieces. Ever since elementary school, I had only one goal in life and it didn't matter what it cost to get there."

"That's unusual clarity and single-mindedness. What was the goal?"

"To become a National Football League player. And finally, last spring, I was recruited."

"That's great news. Congratulations."

Greg's face turned to stone and he shook his head. "That's when it happened," he said. "I had a great spring training and a strong start to the season. But then I got hepatitis." His eyes watered and voice broke. "They hospitalized me. My skin turned yellow."

"I am so sorry," I said.

"It gets worse. The doctor said there was permanent liver damage—that I could never play football again...."

We sat searching each other's eyes for a long minute. I let my face express the shock and sorrow I felt.

Finally, placing my hand over my heart, I said, "This is truly tragic. How have you possibly coped?"

"That's just it," he said. "I haven't. I withdrew from my wife to the point where we hardly talk anymore. I withdrew from the players because it was excruciating to watch them working out. And I withdrew from God because I don't believe he exists any more."

Another silence.

Now I knew why Greg had chosen me. Paradoxically, he had sought out a person of faith in order to confess his loss of faith.

"Greg, I believe you of all people have every right to challenge God's existence," I said. "Do you care to share more about that?"

He nodded. "Yes. I always thought it was God calling me into professional football. I asked his help all the times I felt crushed by opposition or numb with pain. I thought he had big plans for me. And then when I finally became a pro and got my uniform and saw my name on the locker, he gave me hepatitis. What kind of God does that to a child he loves!"

I suddenly felt as helpless as Greg did. I had no answer for God. It would have seemed trite to quote a scripture or ask if he still attended church. At times like this I can wonder why I got into counseling in the first place. Some problems seem too profound to fix.

"So that's why I came to you today," said Greg, breaking through my internal anguish. "I want you to pray for me."

My mind became a freight train: Oh-my-goodness-what-have-I-got-myself-into-I'm-not-supposed-to-witness-to-faith-in-Christ-at-Pepperdine-and-if-this-turns-out-badly-I-could-get-in-big-trouble-with-the-dean!

Fortunately another voice, a calmer one with a different message, whispered within me: *Dan, it's okay to offer a healing prayer when a person asks for spiritual help.*

"All right, Greg," I said. I bowed my head. "Dear Father, you've heard Greg pour out his pain and confusion today. All his hopes have been destroyed; all his dreams shattered. Can you please, in your brilliant capacity for resurrection, restore this young man to a life filled with meaning and fulfillment? I praise you and thank you in Jesus' name, Amen."

I looked up, but Greg still had his head in his hands.

"Greg," I said gently. "Would you like to say a prayer too?"

He hesitated. Then he said, "Oh Lord, I am so sorry I have forsaken you. I never even said goodbye. I just tightened my heart and shut you out. Just like I shut out Marilyn. And all you both ever did was try to love me and help me through life. Please come back to me. Please don't leave me all alone...."

My heart caught. I sat waiting for Greg to finish the prayer. But he didn't, at least not that I could see. Instead, he began to tremble. I thought immediately, *Oh no, I've done it now...I pushed this student over the edge...he's having a panic attack.*

The trembling increased and so did my heart rate, until Greg suddenly sat bolt upright and practically shouted, "I feel him, Dan. I feel God. He is right here with us!"

It took a moment for me to understand that this was no psychotic break, but a glorious visitation by the Mighty Counselor himself.

I watched as Greg looked upward, directly over my head, beaming like a child chucked under the chin—a six-foot-six two hundred and fifty pound young man being hugged and loved by his heavenly Father.

When we did finish up our impromptu session that day, I left Pepperdine appreciating more than ever that we are not alone as pastoral counselors. We are not left fending for ourselves with mere counseling theories and clinical techniques. The Holy Spirit moves where the Spirit wills, and that especially means moving where people are broken and needing one called alongside to help them, one like you or me and the Lord.

When a counselee is moved upon by the grace of God, or experiences the power of the Holy Spirit, there is an afterglow, a fruitfulness of the encounter that remains and grows. For Greg, I noticed an aliveness of interaction with others in the classroom the following week, a new sense of belonging through participation in discussions. An occasional smile or glint in his eyes that told me something was stirring his spirit.

Once again, when class was over, Greg invited me to come and talk to him. After we had seated ourselves in the desks, he said, "Dan, I'll just take a minute of your time, but I want to tell you what's happening."

"Please do," I said.

"First of all, Marilyn and I have been talking all week. I told her about our talk and about how God showed up at the end. She cried with joy, saying she'd been praying for this to happen for many months."

"Wonderful," I said.

"But the amazing thing is that I still feel God with me. It's like I've been hearing this still small voice talking to me all week."

"What is the Lord saying?"

"It's hard to put into words. But I've come to see that I was on the wrong track with the football playing. It had become all about me. And there was no place for God or for my wife. All I wanted was to beat out my teammates so I could play first string and get all the glory."

"That's quite an insight," I said. "I really commend you for hearing it."

"That's not all. It's like I'm receiving a new calling on my life; one I know is coming from God."

"Fascinating. What is it?"

"I think God is calling me to become a high school football coach. When I told Marilyn she said she saw so much potential in me for coaching. She said she felt very relieved because the NFL thing was eating me up."

"Marilyn sounds like a perceptive woman who loves you a lot."

"She is, and now I'm finally loving her back. So anyway, I just want to share that I started back to church with her this weekend and we joined a married couples group."

"Wow."

With a hand big enough to swallow mine, Greg reached across his desk and shook my hand.

"Greg, you're going to become an inspiring coach for a lot of young men—your warmth and enthusiasm are contagious."

"That's my prayer, Dan. That's my hope."

PART III: The Self Compass

10. THE SELF COMPASS GROWTH TOOL

Whether you're looking out upon a sea of faces during the sermon you're delivering, or opening the door of your office to meet the next counselee, the Self Compass growth tool provides a ready aid in understanding all the people you know, including yourself as a pastoral counselor.

What are the dynamics of the Self Compass?

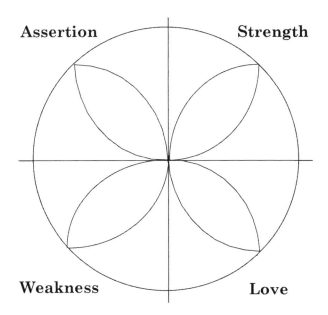

The Self Compass

The Self Compass circle possesses four compass points, much like a physical compass. The compass points are Love and Assertion, Weakness and Strength. Taken together they form the LAWS of personality and relationships.

Think for a moment about one of your counselees. Think about how this person handles love, nurturance, forgiveness, and kindness. This gives you a tentative compass reading on the Love compass point. Now think how the person handles conflict, confrontation, negotiation, and anger. This provides a reading on the Assertion compass point. Now size up that counselee's rhythmic use of Love and Assertion by asking if Love is balanced with Assertion, or if one of these compass points is overly exaggerated or denied.

Next recall how this counselee handles humility, empathy for others, uncertainty, and acknowledgement of deficiencies. This brings perspective about the Weakness compass point. Then check out the Strength compass point, which has to do with expressions of capability, confidence, competence, and achievement. Is either one of these compass points distorted by too much or too little expression, or is there a working rhythm between Weakness and Strength?

Well-balanced persons express caring and kindness with ease (Love), while maintaining the ability to challenge unfairness and negotiate for their reasonable rights (Assertion). Likewise, they are humble enough to admit they have clay feet (Weakness), yet confident enough to enjoy healthy self-esteem (Strength). Hundreds of studies support the *growth psychology* underlying Compass Therapy, indicating that growth in polarity balance offers a reasonable aim for counseling.

For a picture of personality health in action, we can draw upon Christian personality theory (see *Christian Personality Theory: A Self Compass for Humanity*, 2009), and from observing Jesus' behavior in the Gospels. In other words, Christ himself constitutes the behavioral standard against which personality health and personality dysfunction are understood. Let's take a look at some of the dynamics of Christ's attitudes and behavior described in the biblical narrative.

Christ's Self Compass

Indeed, in Jesus' personality and relationships we find the compass rhythms of Love and Assertion. On many occasions he expressed a discerning love for men, women, and children, regardless of their social, financial, educational, or ethnic status. He especially loved Peter, James, John, Martha, Mary, and Lazarus, showing a capacity for heartfelt bonding with those he trusted most. Yet he wasn't indiscriminately loving, as some popular notions portray, for when individuals persisted in arrogance or impenitence, he confronted them, sometimes fiercely, as when driving the moneychangers out of the temple.

So too he expressed healthy rhythms of Weakness and Strength. Though he was God incarnate, he didn't grasp at his divine status, nor use it to avoid pain. Rather, he was a man acquainted with grief (Isa 53:3 NKJV) who learned obedience to God through the things that he suffered (Heb 5:8). Jesus felt the full brunt of the Weakness compass point when he was betrayed into the hands of sinners for crucifixion and death. Nevertheless, he expressed the Strength compass point by preaching the kingdom of God, holding true to the Father's will, and persevering in his mission even when abandoned by friends and followers.

Four biblical titles for Christ illustrate how complimentary opposites form the whole of his personality.

He is the *Good Shepherd*, a helper and healer who gives his life for his sheep (Love compass point); and he is the *Lion of Judah*, a righteous witness against evil and tireless advocate for social justice (Assertion compass point).

He is the *Lamb of God*, who sacrifices his life that humankind might find mercy and forgiveness for sin (Weakness compass point); and he is the *Prince of Peace*, the sovereign Lord of Lords and King of Kings who rightly reigns over the Kingdom of God (Strength compass point).

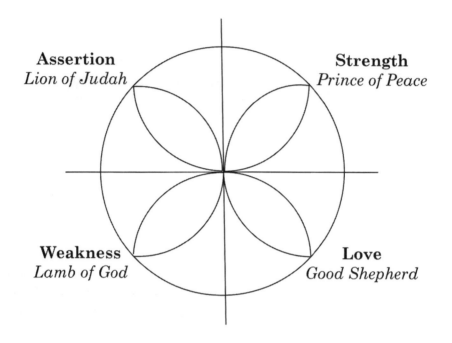

Christ's Self Compass

It is astonishing that even during the ordeal of crucifixion, Jesus still manifests a whole personality, offering words that ring with integrity. "Father, forgive them for they know not what they do" (Love). "John, take care of my mother" (Assertion). "My God, my God, why have you forsaken me?" (Weakness). "It is finished!" (Strength).

Counselees who are growing in Christ learn how to respond to adversity with the self-correcting rhythms of the Self Compass, generating perceptual flexibility and creative problem solving. And if the counselee ascribes to another belief system beyond Christianity, Compass Therapy suggests that compass growth works universally to make the personality more whole.

So you begin to see how this central working model of the Self Compass forms a template for assessing personality dynamics and understanding interpersonal relationships.

Created for Interpersonal Selfhood

There is another dimension of the Self Compass that pertains to all people. The model suggests that human beings are not created for autonomy per se, but rather for meaningful participation in community. Compass Therapy is philosophically grounded in the Holy Trinity as the ontological foundation of human existence. In other words, persons receive their drive for personality and relational fulfillment from God.

The Father, Son, and Holy Spirit are three Persons who radiate the unity of divine love in eternal glory as one God. Since the Trinity has created human beings to know and enter into this divine unity, individuals become healthy to the extent that they develop similitude with God's personality, not only as revealed by Jesus in his earthly life, but by the Father in the history of Israel, by the Holy Spirit after Pentecost, and by the witness of the Word of God in human history.

When you look for this in the Bible you find it: God interacting with humans through a balance of healthy Love and Assertion, Weakness and Strength. And in the healthiest of human responses, say in an Abraham or Moses, a Hannah or Mary, you find a reciprocal responsiveness to God that draws upon Love and Assertion, Weakness and Strength, albeit within the imperfect human frame. Mary, for instance, loves God in her adoration, asserts God's greatness in her Magnificat, surrenders to God's will for her, and has faith that what the angel Gabriel tells her will come to pass. These rhythmic compass relationships reflect the interpersonal selfhood that humans share with God, and that God calls every person to develop.

Thus pastoral ministry and pastoral counseling are primary avenues for helping people perceive what God wants from them, and for releasing them from the traps of personality rigidities, helping them to build a balanced Self Compass as a God-endowed gift for finding their way.

Yet there simultaneously exists the mystery of iniquity, the resistance of sin, the willful use of personality for purposes that undermine and block God's will for health and blessing. Compass Therapy does not hesitate in this regard to include personality rigidities among the "categories of evil" that afflict humankind (Moltmann, 1997, p. 11).

Personality Rigidity

Love that lacks Assertion generates unhealthy dependency upon others, as Paul affirms when he says, "If I were still trying to please people, I would not be a servant of Christ" (Gal 1:10 TNIV). Assertion without the balance of Love results in aggressive behavior that grieves God by hurting others: "Get rid of all bitterness, rage and anger" (Gal 4:31). Strength without Weakness becomes arrogant control, to which God responds, "Whoever has haughty eyes and a proud heart, I will not endure" (Ps 101:5). Weakness without the balance of Strength results in avoidant withdrawal, where a person lives on the sidelines of life, hiding from God and others. "But Jonah ran away from the Lord and headed for Tarshish" (Jon 1:3).

Personality rigidities constrict life in the form of *growth deficiencies* based on ineffective coping patterns (Perls, 1989). Interactions with others become stereotypically repetitive and don't allow for core-to-core sharing on an "I and Thou" basis (Buber, 1970). The predictable rigidity of psychopathology, which reflects the categories of evil, dehumanizes both personality and relationships, including one's relationship with God.

It's not that a person is written off as evil, but rather that good and evil abide within all persons. Personality rigidities tip the scales in the direction of evil, when we understand evil as falling short of the glory of God by making a personality rigidity the paramount force in a person's life—a form of idolatry around which a person organizes thoughts, feelings, sensations, and actions. In fact, compass theory holds that personality patterns cause such harm that one can consider "the center of (moral evil) not as the turbulent appetites, but the personality as a whole" (Trueblood, 1957, p. 251; Bloesch, 2004, p. 52).

I once spoke with Rollo May, the founder of existential psychology, and asked him what he wished that all human beings could know. He reflected for a moment, and then said, "Dan, I would like people to accept that evil isn't something that exists exclusively outside themselves in the world or in others, but rather acts as a force from within, and needs to be owned and worked with if the person is to mature."

Paul had it right when he described himself not as the Chief Apostle, but as the chief of sinners. This acknowledgment that the categories of evil affected him brought with it a profound openness to growth and transformation in Christ.

Personality rigidity opposes the very creativity and genuineness of the Godhead, cutting off individuals from lively and transparent communication with God and others, circumscribing their lives within a constricting range of one or two behavioral responses that are expressed intensely and often, whether or not they are appropriate to a situation (Sullivan, 1954; Shostrom, 1979; Wachtel, 1982; Kiesler, 1996; Montgomery & Montgomery, 2006). This explains why rigid behaviors short-circuit psychospiritual functioning, blocking inspired choices that the Holy Spirit would otherwise offer.

In their essence, personality patterns are not chaotic and random, but specific and predictable. By knowing the location of a personality trend or pattern on the Self Compass, the pastoral counselor gains x-ray vision into its structure and function, and can logically deduce its antidote. That is, by understanding a particular pattern's rhyme and reason, you foresee how to transform its growth-resistant rigidity into a rhythm of actualizing health (Tracey, 2005; Montgomery, 2008).

A Diagnosis-to-Growth Model

Over seventy-five years of personality research from an interpersonal perspective has developed a consensus regarding what constitutes personality, supporting the notion of a growth continuum that connects the compass model of personality health with personality dysfunction. If you are interested in the integration of this research with biblical theology and essential Christian doctrine, I refer you to *Compass Psychotheology: Where Psychology & Theology Really Meet* (Montgomery & Montgomery, 2006).

In the application of Compass Therapy to pastoral counseling, strategies for intervention emerge from diagnosing where a person is stuck on the Self Compass, and formulating goals for transforming personality deficiencies into actualizing growth. This allows pastoral counselors a degree of warranted optimism. Alfred Adler writes, "The construction of a goal premises the capacity for change, and a certain freedom of movement. The spiritual enrichment which results is not to be undervalued" (1927/1965, p. 44).

As counseling progresses, counselees develop increments of freedom that increase their flexibility and adaptability. Stagnant patterns lose their grip as counselees take experimental growth stretches into unused compass points where they discover more gratifying outcomes.

How then do we begin?

11. THE TRENDS & PATTERNS SELF COMPASS

The Self Compass not only shows counselees how to integrate the four compass points into their personality and relationships, but also reveals what happens when they are "stuck" on a compass point. A rigid personality *trend* arrests actualizing growth, stranding a counselee in a lifestyle characterized by too much dependency, too much aggression, too much withdrawal, or too much control—or a combination of these trends. These distortions affect self-functioning and impinge upon interpersonal relationships.

If the counselee has a spiritual orientation, these trends undercut its effectiveness by seeing God as Pollyannaish and syrupy sweet (Love compass point), wrathful and persecutory (Assertion compass point), aloof or emotionally absent (Weakness compass point), or authoritarian and dictatorial (Strength compass point). For a fuller treatment of counselee images of God, see *Christian Counseling That Really Works* (Montgomery, 2006).

Rigid behavior often begins in childhood as recurring attempts to ward off anxiety. For instance, a shy child avoids the Strength compass point by collapsing into Weakness, or an aggressive child exaggerates Assertion and avoids Love.

During pastoral counseling you can develop an intelligible explanation for the origin of fixation on a particular compass point, though in most cases the root cause involves a a combination of genetic predisposition, traumatic experiences, the arresting of psychosocial development, and spiritual stagnation that disrupts normal growth and shunts an individual's concentration from flexible coping to defensive self-protection. Compass Therapy's view of rigid trends as growth deficiencies carries with it the invitation for actualizing growth, thereby generating hope for counselees.

Using the Trends Self Compass with Counselees

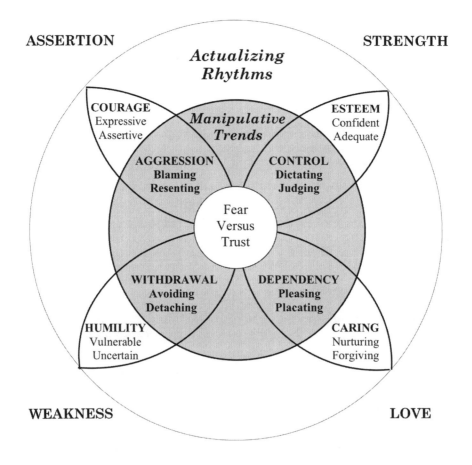

Trends Self Compass

There are four manipulative trends located on the Self Compass. Carl Jung, Alfred Adler, Harry Stack Sullivan, Karen Horney, Virginia Satir, Everett Shostrom, and Aaron Beck, among other counseling theorists, have in their own way described these trends as dependency, aggression, withdrawal, and compulsive control.

Notice how the outer circle of the Trends Self Compass describes the healthy compass points in their actualizing expression. Moving around the compass in clockwise fashion, the counselee sees that actualizing Love fosters nurturing and forgiving. Healthy Weakness expresses vulnerability and uncertainty. Diplomatic Assertion offers expressiveness and assertiveness. Humble Strength yields confidence and adequacy. You can point out that personality and relational health results when these polarities are expressed rhythmically and in dynamic balance.

Next, the pastoral counselor describes how the shaded circle reveals the unconscious hidden agenda that governs each trend. This circle is smaller than the actualizing circle and bordered by a thicker ring to indicate that manipulative trends contract the personality, constricting freedom by diminishing creativity. You point out, too, that trust in the spiritual core, that center of reflective consciousness where the person engages and is engaged by the Holy Spirit, is now overshadowed by core fear, the driving force that underlies the distress of manipulative living.

By now counselees are thinking about how these descriptions might pertain to them and their troubles. They'll also want to understand what the word "manipulative" means.

"You manipulate yourself and others when you're feeling sad but acting happy, as though nothing is wrong," you might say. "Or when you hate something but say you love it." You find your own way of helping the counselee grasp that fear-driven behavior results in incongruence, where thoughts don't match feelings or body language, and where persons lose touch with what is really going on inside them.

While everyone is occasionally dependent or aggressive or withdrawn or controlling, a manipulative trend congeals into a fixated way of life that has dehumanizing repercussions (Adler, 1927/1965; Montgomery & Montgomery, 2007).

"How does this relate to the LAWS and the Self Compass?" the counselee may ask.

You take a quick trip around the compass, summarizing these universal manipulations. "If we're stuck on the Love compass point, we're too nice to everyone and become dependent. We please and placate others, and forget about ourselves. If we're stuck in Weakness, we withdraw from life to avoid situations that make us uncomfortable. We solve anxiety by detaching from people. If we overdo the Assertion compass point, we get mad a lot. We blame others for our aggression and resent them for making us angry. And if too much Strength is our issue, we try to control everything by dictating how life should be and judging people when they keep falling short. By balancing all these compass points we gain the advantage of the best that each has to offer."

The counselee nods, taking a closer look at the Self Compass. "I think I see myself in there."

"All right," you say, handing over the diagram. "Where do you see yourself and how do you suppose you got there?"

This productive direction heightens counselee awareness of how a particular trend creates interference. By talking about it, they make the trend more *ego-dystonic*, or distanced from themselves, rather than *ego-syntonic*, or merged with themselves. Gradually, counselees come to understand that a manipulative trend is a temporary behavioral template they can outgrow—a skewed way of functioning they can replace. Recognizing how they are manipulating self and others brings with it the freedom to choose otherwise.

Personality Patterns

In this category of personality rigidity, pervasive lifestyles sown from the root system of manipulative trends have rigidified into differentiated *patterns* that are nevertheless amenable to growth and change. You can readily remember them by their location on the Self Compass. I am giving an overview now, but will address each in the following chapters that include guidelines for counseling intervention.

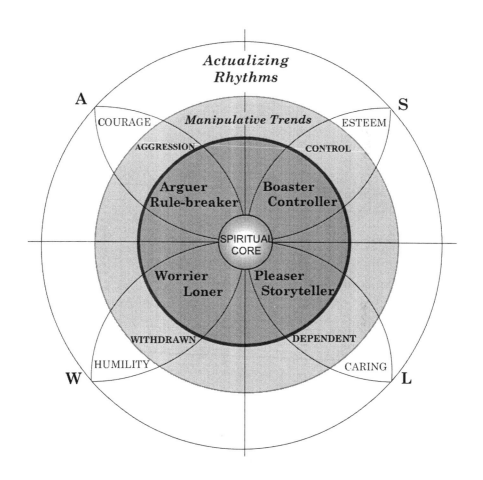

Patterns Self Compass

✤ The *dependent Pleaser* and *histrionic Storyteller* patterns are located on the Love compass point, where the dependent trend intensifies into chronic pleasing and placating (dependent) or melodramatic craving for attention (histrionic). Both patterns share intense needs for approval and affection (Millon & Grossman, 2007a), as well as a fixated focus on others that blocks access to the spiritual core.

✢ The *paranoid Arguer* and *antisocial Rule-breaker* patterns are stuck on the Assertion compass point, where the aggressive trend develops into edgy suspicion (paranoid) or impenitent exploitation (antisocial). These two patterns frequently "co-vary as personality mixtures" (Millon & Grossman, 2007b, p. 203), and share an undercurrent of hostility (Beck et al., 2007). They typically consider others as adversaries over whom they must triumph (Montgomery & Montgomery, 2006).

✢ The *avoidant Worrier* and *schizoid Loner* patterns are located on the Weakness compass point, where the withdrawn trend intensifies into fearful loneliness (avoidant) or isolated detachment (schizoid). Both patterns create flat affect, a lack of motivation in personal development, and massive deficiencies in interpersonal skills (West et al., 1995).

✢ The *narcissistic Boaster* and *compulsive Controller* patterns are lodged on the Strength compass point, where striving for superiority pushes the controlling trend into either the grandiose entitlement of the narcissist or the judgmental perfectionism of the compulsive (Montgomery, 2008). These two patterns share a common preoccupation with the issues of "adequacy, power, and prestige" (Millon & Grossman, 2007a, p. 271). Both patterns are quite comfortable taking control and dictating (Beck et al., 2007). Both patterns share the demand for perfection, the narcissist seeking the glory of ambition and the compulsive enforcing the status quo (Millon et al., 2004, p. 357).

Actualizing Health

The Self Compass offers a range of resourceful behaviors that help counselees make creative choices that gradually dismantle constricting trends and patterns.

At the actualizing level (shown on the Patterns Self Compass diagram), counselees learn to relate with a relatively high degree of self-awareness and interpersonal discernment, the growth aim of all therapeutic strategies.

With the LAWS of personality as their guide, they learn how to express love for someone without letting that person take advantage. They selectively assert themselves if someone seeks to manipulate them, yet recover without falling back into chronic defensiveness. They discover how to form core-to-core relationships characterized by "I and Thou" respectfulness, while reserving the right to protect themselves against all forms of manipulation.

As the Love and Assertion compass points are informed by one another, they yield virtues of *caring* and *courage*. The synergy of Weakness with Strength results in the virtues of *humility* and *esteem* for self and others. These complementary virtues develop from within, knit together by the spiritual core.

The spiritual core of personality acts as a person's center of gravity (Horney, 1945); inner locus of control (Rogers, 1961); nuclear atom in the total psychic system (Jung, 1968); inner supreme court (Maslow, 1971); higher self (Assagioli, 2000); spiritual self (Frankl, 2006); and the "I am" center of awareness and free agency (Montgomery & Montgomery, 2006). Strengthening a counselee's trust in the spiritual core during the counseling process generates hope, self-efficacy, and resiliency (Stajkovic, 2006).

The Compass Model provides a working overview for transforming rigidity in the direction of personality wholeness and effective relationships. Actualizing development takes form in a manner unique to every counselee. Gradual progress toward wholeness is the aim.

Compass theory asserts that no one is immune from some degree of personality rigidity, which is part of the human condition. Yet a counselee can make substantial gains toward psychological and spiritual maturity (Andrews, 1991). The cadenced, self-correcting polarities of the LAWS of personality form a solid basis for a resilient self-identity that allows counselees to find their core selves and develop a center that holds.

Now for a closer look at these patterns and how to approach them in both counseling and church settings. (For those interested, the Appendix includes research summaries regarding each pattern that support and enhance Clinical Pastoral Education).

12. Love Stuck: Pleaser & Storyteller

While Christianity promotes the value of love above all human qualities, love actually becomes a problem for people who love too much. This is not common knowledge in churches, so the pastoral counselor who understands the difference between healthy and unhealthy expressions of love helps both counselees and the whole congregation.

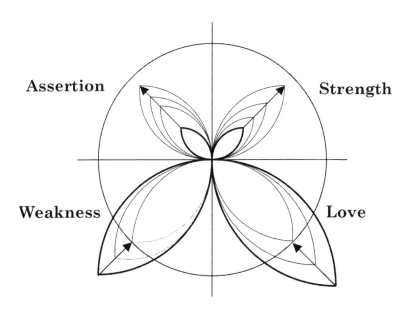

Pleaser and Storyteller Self Compass

The Love stuck patterns of the *dependent Pleaser* and the *histrionic Storyteller* are unhealthy because of the great need for approval and acceptance from others. Notice in the skewed Self Compass how the Love compass point is pushed out beyond the self-circle, revealing that the counselee exaggerates love and thereby distorts its meaning. This exaggeration exerts a force on the Weakness compass point as well, making it more inflated than is healthy. Likewise both the Assertion and Strength compass points are truncated, which means they are denied healthy expression.

What are the personal and interpersonal consequences of being stuck with too much love?

There is an undercurrent of anxiety, guilt feelings, and insecurity about where one stands with others and with God. This comes from the nagging need to make others happy and the bothersome fear that someone might show disapproval. Yet these feelings are kept under the carpet of consciousness, since becoming aware of them would tarnish the image of being a loving person. The principal at work here is that compass points which are most exaggerated are most identified with the person's consciousness, while those compass points most denied are exiled to the unconscious. This is why pastoral counselors do well to penetrate surface behavior with x-ray vision into the unconscious depths, guiding counselees to increase awareness and expression of their whole Self Compass.

Once you grasp that Love stuck counselees don't yet realize that many of their personal and interpersonal frustrations arise from letting people take advantage of them, then you intuitively understand that growth stretches into the Assertion and Strength compass points (as shown by the arrows in the diagram) will bring the maturity they need.

Christ never intended love to make his disciples bereft of personal identity or obsessed with pleasing those around them. Peter would have never preached such a firm and challenging sermon on the day of Pentecost if the Holy Spirit had turned him into a people-pleaser who wanted to keep the peace at all costs. But the Holy Spirit had the opposite effect, making Peter a more mature person who could love others while at the same time confronting them when necessary, as he did in this historic sermon (Acts 2:14-40).

As we move through this chapter I will begin to differentiate the dependent Pleaser pattern from the histrionic Storyteller pattern, so that you can understand why they are both stuck on Love, yet in two different ways. Fundamentally, the dependent Pleaser is soft-spoken, gentle, caring, kind, and self-effacing, needing people's approval without making a show of it. By contrast, the histrionic Storyteller is high-strung, flamboyant, theatrical, seductive, and petulant in an overt effort to capture people's love and rivet their attention.

Here are typical thoughts and assumptions that characterize Love-stuck counselees prior to personality transformation.

Love-Stuck Thoughts:

Pleaser: (For research, see Appendix, pp. 204-206).

⊕ I'm responsible for the happiness of others.

⊕ I should never offend another person.

⊕ I must keep the peace at all costs.

⊕ I should take everyone's problems to heart.

⊕ It is selfish to think of my own needs.

⊕ If I'm nice to them, others will like me.

⊕ I must keep my real feelings to myself.

Storyteller: (For research, see Appendix, pp. 206-208).

✦ Unless I captivate people's attention I am nothing.

✦ I am irresistible and deserve special love.

✦ It's not my fault I'm forgetful and disorganized. I just get caught up in the spontaneity of life!

✦ People will abandon me if I'm not the life of the party.

✦ If I don't entertain people or flirt with them, they'll find me boring.

✦ I am very intuitive about people.

Pleaser Counselees

In a first counseling session, you can feel the pressure Pleaser counselees are under to make a favorable impression. You accommodate this need because you want the person to feel at home and come to trust you. Yet before long, at least by a second session, you'll want to begin disclosing this pattern, so that the pattern doesn't take charge of the counseling by turning you into a "nice counselor" who does them little good.

So the task of the pastoral counselor becomes two-fold: to provide a measure of attention and approval these counselees need, while conveying that the counseling process includes receiving feedback about their pattern that will ultimately help them solve a host of personal and interpersonal problems.

In a first session Janet has shared that she feels depressed and can't figure out why. By the middle of the session you have discerned that she is run ragged by the narcissistic demands of her husband and two adolescent boys, whom you sense have a pattern of taking from her without giving anything back.

You say, "Janet, I believe there are some dynamics in your personality that are setting you up for this depression. Somehow you've made yourself a personal servant to three family members who are perfectly capable of doing many things for themselves, but that you are doing for them."

"But I want to be a loving wife and mother," protests Janet. "Doesn't that mean making my family happy?"

"I know that you are a very loving wife and mother. Yet I wonder if your personality hasn't been unconsciously programmed to carry this theme too far."

"What do you mean?"

"I mean that being loving to family members or anyone else only equals half of the equation for a healthy relationship. The other half involves standing up for yourself when they expect too much and taking just as much care of yourself as you do for them."

"But that sounds selfish. I want to put my family first, and serve the Lord by serving them."

"I think it's great that Christ is your model. But let me ask you something. Did Jesus serve the disciples by making them his boss?"

"No."

"Did he run himself ragged looking out for their needs and making them happy?"

"No."

"Why not?"

"I suppose it's because they would have taken advantage of him. You know, made him waste his time by doing everything they wanted."

(Because you are guiding the conversation in a way that evokes Janet's imagination, this allows her to project her life story onto Jesus, but with a greater truth that she unconsciously knows: that pleasing and placating only makes others more demanding).

"So what did he do instead?"

"Well, he had boundaries with them, where he would show them love but also tell them when they were wrong-headed."

"So he didn't love them to the point of kowtowing to them and putting them in charge of his life, but rather balanced his love with assertion when he needed to confront them. Is that right?"

"Yes, otherwise they would have driven him crazy."

"Janet, that is a profound theological and psychological insight and I want to commend you for it."

(This lavish praise both meets Janet's interior need to be viewed positively and thought well of, and also reinforces her spontaneous use of the Assertion and Strength compass points, whereby she has articulated a richer perception of Christ than her Love stuck compass would normally allow).

"So are you telling me that I'm too much of a pushover with my family?"

"That is a powerful way of expressing the dilemma of the dependent Pleaser pattern. How else would you apply this insight to your present situation?"

"Well, my husband does expect me to wait on him hand and foot. Honestly, one of my friends told me that he's my third child. Yet he's so sure of himself that I'm afraid to question his expectations. He thinks I should work at a job as well as raise the kids, and do all the cooking and house-work and bill paying without bothering him about it."

"How does he reward you for such luxurious service?"

Janet frowns. "He doesn't criticize me as much when I do everything for him."

"No wonder you feel depressed!"

With this kind of counseling interaction, Janet remains free to explore her thoughts, feelings, and puzzlements, with an assurance that the counseling is headed somewhere pro-ductive. She's not seeing you just to ventilate her secret pain or cry on your shoulder, because you are making it clear that the Compass Therapy approach to pastoral counseling will offer her a new foundation for living.

Precisely because you are not inviting her into long-term psychotherapy, but rather into short-term counseling and coaching, you say, "I'd like to encourage you to begin reading a book before our next session. It's called *The Self Compass* and the purpose of reading it is to discover where you locate your personality, and your husband and sons' personalities on the Self Compass. This growth tool is anchored in Scripture and Christ's own personality, and will help us make more rapid progress than we would otherwise."

This may seem like a lot to cover in a first or second session, but one of the features of Compass Therapy is the straightforward introduction of compass concepts and the Self Compass growth tool as active agents for growth and transformation. It is your very mastery of compass theory that gives you the expertise to guide counseling, including question-asking and other methods, along productive lines that get to the core of the person's problems, which always have to do with the structure of their personality.

Storyteller Counselee

Now let's look at an example that centers on the histrionic Storyteller pattern. A fellow pastor asks for a counseling session with you, and once you've begun the session, he says, "I'm here because I want to share something I've never told anyone, even though I experienced it in seminary and I haven't gotten over it in ten years of pastoring, and it has to do with this pressure I feel to always make a big impact on people and get their emotional motivation going and come up with things in my sermons that keeps everybody on the edge of their seats..."

As Wayne gulps for breath you sit forward in your chair, discerning that he may be living in the grip of the Storyteller pattern, unaware of the emotional rollercoaster this pattern exerts. In responding, you want to somewhat match the ramped-up delivery style and dramatic speech that drives the Storyteller pattern. Otherwise the pattern will bury you and the counselee in stories that don't stop long enough for comment or reflection.

"Okay, Wayne," you say, putting enough energy in your voice to command his attention. "It sounds like there's this secret part of your personality that you've hidden from people for years, a part that is actually very anxious to make an excellent impression. Is that right?"

"Absolutely. In my sermons, I have to make sure I make eye contact with every person in every row and I have to have an ending that brings tears or laughter, but if anyone yawns, it's a disaster and I take it all so personally..."

You allow Wayne to talk for several minutes in his rapid paced free association style, not getting lost in all the stories because you're observing his histrionic way of living and relating. You summarize what he's said in a positive way, and then shift the focus.

"So it's like preaching and teaching means a great deal to you, yet it always brings an anxiety that you'd like to lessen."

"That's right."

"Wayne, what do you feel in your body right now?"

(This deliberate change from the Heart to the Body begins a process of helping Wayne knit together his whole human nature, a process that can ultimately bring more serenity than anxiety to his spiritual core).

Wayne rubs his solar plexus, the nerve center below the breastbone. "My heart is beating kind of fast, and there's a knot here like a tight fist that leaves me kind of breathless."

"And if we give this knot a voice, what does it say?"

Wayne reflects for a moment. "It says, 'I need everybody to feel excited about what I'm saying and get on board with my program...so I can believe in myself.'"

(It is amazing how much people really know that has never congealed into consciousness. When the unconscious

116

comes up with an existential statement like this, you thank the unconscious and summarize the wisdom embedded in the statement in order to make it more conscious).

"I want to thank your unconscious for coming up with such an authentic statement. I wonder if it's trying to tell you that your inner center of gravity—the center of your personality—is too leveraged out onto other people. That perhaps you need people's approval so much that it hurts."

Wayne looks off into space, then back at you. "I think you've hit on something, because the knot's loosening a little."

"What happens when you don't command people's full attention?"

He sighs. "I feel like I disappear, like I'm not significant—just the other day..."

(You raise your hand to stop him, because if you don't, he can fill the rest of the session with non-stop story recitation fueled by the very pattern you are helping him to recognize and outgrow). "May I offer a tentative hypothesis that might lead to a counseling goal?"

"Okay," he says, reigning himself in and sinking back into his chair.

"It seems to me that your personality might be overly influenced by the histrionic Storyteller pattern as your main way of getting on in the world. It seems to solve your interpersonal anxiety by making people very interested in you. But you're seeing now how this pattern hardly lets you breathe. It's always planning a next story to tell or some other dramatic way to hold someone's attention."

Wayne purses his lips. "My wife says I'm a non-stop talker. And now that I think of it, my old homiletics professor said I could use less drama and more substance. But that's where I always lose it. When I've got a captive audience, I just can't help ramping up the energy until they're on the edge of their seats..."

"Just like you're starting to do now?"

Wayne smiles and sits back in his chair. "Right."

"So can we agree on the therapeutic goals of increasing relaxation in your body, and learning how to communicate with less drama and more substance?"

Wayne laughs. "I'd like that very much, but I don't know how to live without high drama. Just the other day…"

In counseling Pleasers and Storytellers, you keep the conversation going in ways that respond to their here and now needs, while pacing the sessions to include insights and "growth stretches" into the Assertion and Strength compass points, deliberately not reinforcing over-reliance on the Love and Weakness compass points. Whether you are seeing counselees for three or thirteen or thirty sessions, you are helping them learn to recognize the holes in their personality and fill these with a more flexible use of the whole Self Compass.

In terms of the Human Nature Compass, Pleasers and Storytellers favor the Heart dimension, because they experience a lot of anxiety and seek the emotional comfort of total acceptance from other people. Since this extreme other-direction blocks inner serenity, you foster greater engagement of the Mind to help them adopt more rational and autonomous beliefs, the Body to develop a relaxation response through abdominal breathing and muscle melting, and the Spirit to evolve a more visceral surrender to the Holy Spirit that increases their inner peace in Christ.

13. ASSERTION STUCK: ARGUER & RULE-BREAKER

In Compass Therapy, the Assertion compass point lies opposite the Love compass point. Compass theory predicts that Assertion-stuck patterns manifest aggression and suspicion at the expense of caring and vulnerability.

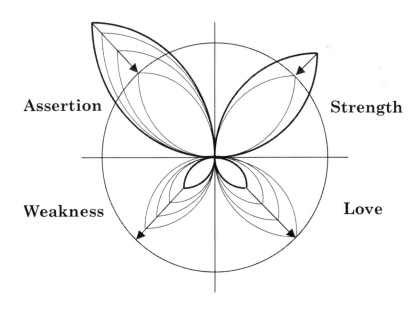

The Arguer and Rule-breaker Self Compass

Notice that the skewed Self Compass of the *antisocial Rule-breaker* and *paranoid Arguer* patterns pushes the Assertion compass point out beyond the Self Compass circle, revealing the predominance of anger and social distrust embedded in those stuck with too much aggression. This overbearing assertion exerts pressure on the Strength compass point as well, moving it out of bounds, meaning that Rule-breakers and Arguers aren't just conniving, but arrogant about getting their way. The collapsed Weakness and Love compass points indicate a lack of either humility or caring for others.

By following the direction of the arrows within each compass point, you can see how the strategic aim of pastoral counseling lies in diminishing overly exaggerated Assertion and Strength, and expanding under-expressed Weakness and Love, working toward overall compass balance.

Aggressive counselees exemplify why pastoral counselors cannot afford naivety about personality patterns. Such individuals have the power and proclivity to actually use counseling against you. In the Gospel narrative, Judas reveals both the Arguer and Rule-breaker patterns in his personality, and these bring him not only to resist Christ's influence on his interior life, but also use Jesus' teaching against him. The fact that the Bible doesn't leave out Judas's avarice and betrayal, but rather highlights it, shows that pastoral counselors need the ability to recognize this pattern and deal with it wisely.

One of the best ways to neutralize a counselee's pattern is to know in advance the thoughts and assumptions the pattern creates in the counselee. Here are some examples.

Assertion-Stuck Thoughts

Arguer: (For research, see Appendix, pp. 208-210).

 ✤ People can't be trusted because they are devious and will side against you.

- I am honest in saying that my philosophy of life is how things really are.

- I must test those around me to see if they are loyal.

- Other people want to interfere with my freedom, put me down, and discriminate against me. I have never received the good treatment that society owes me.

- If people seem friendly, they're only trying to manipulate me. I need constant vigilance against adversaries who want to take advantage of me.

- I am hard-nosed and proud of it. People make me angry because they are untrustworthy and exasperating.

Rule-breaker: (For research, see Appendix, pp. 210-212).

- I disdain traditional ideals and hold conventional ethics in contempt (Blair et al., 2005).

- I have no guilt about using and discarding others when I no longer need them.

- I take pleasure in shrewdness, calculation, and the transgression of social codes (Martens, 2005).

- I'll never be caught because I'm too smart.

- I can wear a mask of helpful civility to hide my true intentions (Salekin et al., 2005).

- I don't mind escalating into verbal threats or physical violence if it gets me what I want.

- I think people should have access to all the alcohol and drugs they want.

- Openness and caring are signs of weakness. If I run into a kind and attentive counselor, I'll "take him (or her) for a ride" (Benjamin, 2003, p. 212).

You notice that a person trapped in aggression lacks a normal degree of transparency and openness in communication. Rather, there is a sense of calculated brusqueness, of quickly paced comebacks, vying for control of the conversation by holding back elements of the self. In other words, the aggressive person is constantly looking you over, watching for your weaknesses, sizing you up in ways that wouldn't even occur to people who balance Assertion with Love, and Strength with Weakness.

Compass theory explains this as withholding the Heart and Spirit dimensions of human nature in order to calculate with the Mind and tightly control the Body language. In fact, Assertion stuck counselees show discomfort in a counseling session because they want to turn the tables by taking charge of the process and outcome of pastoral counseling.

Arguer Counselees

Arguer-patterned individuals frequently seek counseling because someone close to them is not doing their will and they don't like it. They adopt a charming persona with a pastoral counselor to paint themselves in the best possible light, seeking to recruit agreement that they are in the right and the person they're complaining about is in the wrong.

An example of the Arguer is the husband who says, "I've tried my best to be the spiritual leader of our family. But my wife insists on not obeying me. Not only that, but she disagrees with how I want to raise the kids. I was wondering if you could have a talk with her and straighten her out."

If you try to challenge this ironclad rule about his family, he can turn against you in a moment and give you a blast of temper, and later, beyond the counseling experience, bad mouth you to others in the congregation. Yet challenging the aggressive pattern offers his only hope for outgrowing the habit of bullying those who rely upon him.

So how do you handle an Arguer counselee?

First of all, realize that God is asking himself the same question and does have a redemptive plan, if only the Arguer will cooperate. Second, you can reflect the Arguer's emotions without being recruited into collusion against another person outside of counseling. And third, you can fairly quickly show that you see through the Arguer tactic for ruling relationships through suspicion, cynicism, or intimidation; you reveal your immunity to their pattern's wiles.

How?

By giving up your need to help this counselee much until the person begins to reveal deeper emotions and demonstrates motivation for growth and change.

I first met Don in a Christian College counseling center shortly after I arrived there. He was hard to miss, skulking around campus like a lion seeking his next meal. When he dropped into my office, I wondered if he had come to make mincemeat out of me.

I knew in advance that Don had an agenda for arguing, because some professors had confided to me how they hated when he signed up for their courses. Even the president of the college had told me that Don was spoiling the campus atmosphere.

By using his intimidating attitude, as well as exploiting his presence as the only Native-American on campus, Don had found a perfect way to establish his identity through negative attention-getting behavior. As a consequence, people walked on eggshells around him.

The first words out of his mouth were, "I think psychologists are full of crap."

(Knowing that Arguers thrive on arguing, I didn't take the bait).

I nodded with interest and said, "Do you suppose Ph.D. really means 'piled higher and deeper?'"

He laughed. "Whatever. But no one is ever going to tell me what to do."

"That's a very succinct philosophy of life."

"Well, aren't you going to try to fix me?"

"You seem happy with yourself. What's there to fix?"

"Everybody says I have a bad temper."

"What do you think about that?"

"I think I speak my mind and I'm not afraid of anybody."

"You say that with relish, as though you really enjoy challenging people."

"This whole college keeps trying to shut me up, but I won't let them."

"It's like you're a lone warrior who is fierce and fearless, and you won't back down from anyone."

(This surprise comment aligned me with Don's inner self, something he clearly wasn't used to).

"Well, yes, you might say so."

(Now Don was at a loss for words; his narrow interpersonal script didn't allow room for compliments from the Love compass point or dignifying statements from Strength).

"So tell me, Don, what is a man like you doing at a college like this?"

"First off, it's a free ride because the government's paying my tab. And second, I like a place where I can bat people against the wall. Christianity is stupid that way, teaching people to be weak and sniveling so that they end up spineless."

(This was a fine statement of Don's cynicism, a perfectly articulated bottom line of the Arguer pattern. But since this was a real person talking, and not just a pattern, I wanted to expand the humanness of his perspective, to show respect for it, and see where it might take us. Notice how I refused to fall into an argumentative repartee).

"So might I assume that one of your positive values has to do with Christians developing more courage to stand up for their convictions, so they're not just jellyfish who anybody can step on?"

"Exactly! If people would stand up to me I wouldn't push them around so much. I'm really not an evil guy. I just want people to have guts and I hate it when they're nicey-nice."

We carried on this way for a while longer, and then I said, "Well, Don, we're about out of time. We need to set a growth goal if you want to keep talking to me."

"You mean you're so high and mighty that I can't just come in here to shoot the bull?"

"You can shoot the bull if we're at the cafeteria. But if you want to see me here in the counseling center, you've got to deliver more of yourself than just spouting off."

(I knew this was a challenge, but aggressive persons need social boundaries that are fairly and firmly enforced. Even if he got mad and walked out the door, I was going to stand up for my right to speak forthrightly just like I had championed his right to do so).

Don grinned. "You're the only person I've let talk to me like that since I've been here. Okay, I'd like to come in again. What do I have to do?"

Don committed to a course of short-term counseling. In the second session I heard more of his history and evolved an understanding of why he'd developed such an outspoken chip on the shoulder. By the third session I was talking to him about the Self Compass, showing him why too much aggression was making it impossible for him to give and receive love, and how this predicted a life of lonely alienation, riddled with resentments and empty within. Don had his automatic pilot comebacks and bristled with confrontation now and then. I stayed firm with my criteria that seeing me for sessions required peeling the onion of his personality. He stayed with the process.

By a fifth session I noticed Don engaging in more genuine exchanges with people in the Quad outside my office, instead of scowling and prowling around. This is when I said, "You know, Don, I think you have a remarkable way with people now that you don't turn everything into a fight."

He smiled even while shrugging it off, as if he didn't care about such things. "People are showing me more respect."

In the sixth session I summarized his progress. "It seems to me like you're really solving the riddle of relationships by listening to other people instead of verbally stalking them. How are you managing that, since I know you could bite off their heads at any moment?"

"I think I feel more comfortable inside myself," he said, giving me a sincere look I'd not seen before. "It's like my old anger isn't there so much. I'm starting to like a few people."

"I've noticed. What's that like?"

"It's like I don't have to take on the world anymore. And some people seem to like me."

"Count me as one of them."

I closed that last session, saying, "Come back anytime."

I think on balance that Don's journey into a richer way of experiencing life than the paranoid Arguer pattern allows shows that no one has to remain beyond the pale of redemptive growth and transformation. And the fact that the whole college community entered a new level of calmness showed that one person's willingness to transform his aggravating and divisive influence could significantly improve an entire social environment. This is why a pastoral counselor does well to become fearless and skilled in working to neutralize the paranoid Arguer pattern.

Rule-breaker Counselees

The antisocial Rule-breaker pattern is either kept well hidden, or else shamelessly glorified through a prominent leadership position. In the first instance, a counselee secretly struggles with lying, gambling, stealing, conning, extramarital affairs, or addiction. In the second instance the Rule-breaker is what Scripture calls a wolf in sheep's clothing, as when a pastor raises funds for building a new church and when all the money is collected, leaves town.

The hallmark of the pattern lies in its exploitive attitude toward other people and an inability, or perhaps unwillingness, to feel guilt about it.

While Rule-breakers in general avoid pastoral counseling, the pattern can crop up mixed with other personality patters. Recognizing it can help a counselee dismantle its interior influence, assuming there is willingness to do so.

First, though, let's examine what the pattern promises the person who adopts it. Have you ever noticed that when directly confronted about wrongdoing, children often look guilty but quickly make up a story that gets them off the hook? They are experimenting with lying, and as a result can discover that telling a lie works better than the truth, because if they don't get caught, there is no shame or punishment.

Likewise children and adolescents often experiment with sex, stealing, drugs, alcohol, and cruelty to certain peers. Antisocial adults continue to carry on these experiments, even though the stakes are raised by the contexts of employment, marriage, church membership, and state or federal laws. The pattern promises them that they will not get caught; that there is excitement in risk-taking; that normative laws don't apply to their behavior; and that the pleasure of the moment is more intriguing than discipline or perseverance.

As a pastoral counselor you cannot afford to be naïve about human experimental behavior, because the church organist may be having sex with the choir director despite the fact that they are both married with children, the church treasurer may be cooking the books, and that suave fellow that the pastor has put in charge of greeting people at Sunday service may be selling them worthless insurance policies on the side.

Expect to hear anything and everything in your counseling career, and you'll be fine. And when counselees disclose the earmarks of antisocial behavior, start thinking in compass terms.

When you hear how your counselee has used his brother's credit card to charge several thousand dollars worth of items in the past two years, you don't want to blanch or give a moralistic lecture. Nor do you want to take a purely empathetic stance, implying that individuals are the product of their environment and can't help the way they behave.

Compass Therapy navigates a middle course by encouraging reflection of the counselee's disclosures, coupled with objective statements about how personality patterns exact heavy tolls on personal happiness.

For instance, Angela has come into pastoral counseling and told you that her husband is sick of her lying behavior. He has mentioned the possibility of a divorce.

You empathize with her pain, probe to find out what the pattern of lying is all about, and then summarize toward the end of the session.

"So Angela, it seems that this reflex tendency to color the facts and lead people to certain conclusions that aren't true started with lying to your father about having sex with your boyfriend in high school. It seems like you didn't fully realize how covering up the truth would become a pattern in your personality, but apparently that's what your husband has discovered. Am I on the right track?"

Angela looks uncomfortable. "Yes, I suppose. I can't stop lying even when I promise myself I won't do it again. It just keeps happening. And Frank is very bitter about it."

"It's like you dearly want a loving relationship with Frank, but you're finding out that the Rule-breaker pattern is sabotaging it. Somehow the pattern makes you think you can pull off lying about spending, even though objectively you know you can't."

"That's true. But I keep thinking I can hide it anyway."

"In spite of the fact that you're about to lose Frank over this issue."

Angela tears slightly. (This is why watching body language is so important. This little sign of remorse offers a ray of hope, since normally the antisocial pattern is devoid of a conscience). "I simply have to change, but I'm afraid I can't."

"I wonder if you're willing to transform that fear into a prayer."

She looks surprised. "You mean right now?"

"Yes, a prayer to the Lord to grant you a willing heart for growth and change, because you don't see much hope on your own."

"Okay."

You bow your head and so does she.

"Dear Lord," says Angela, "please help me. I want Frank to love me, but I'm the one who's driving him away. I've been lying for so long I don't know how not to. Please forgive me and help me find my way."

You come in with a consolidating prayer. "We thank you, Father, for being with us in our counseling sessions. Bring us wisdom that gives Angela personality growth that overcomes the urge to lie. In Jesus' name, Amen."

At your next session, Angela comes in carrying *The Self Compass* book and when you've started, says, "The inventory in this book showed a high score on the Rule-breaker pattern, but just as high on the Pleaser pattern. And when I read the Pleaser chapter it described the need I have to always be seen in a positive light and not to upset anybody."

"This is fascinating, Angela, because it means your personality is caught between two opposing patterns, and this accounts for why you have such a blind spot around lying to Frank about money."

"I'm feeling anxious just talking about it."

"That's good, actually, because it means you've got a conscience. Now tell me a little about this need to please others."

"I just can't stand to disappoint anyone. And I can't stand the idea of them being angry with me—which is exactly what happens every time Frank finds out I've lied about spending too much."

"It's like the part of you that's stuck in the Pleaser pattern doesn't want to upset Frank about your Rule-breaker spending. So you keep everything to yourself until suddenly the ax falls."

Angela sighs. "That's how I live. What should I do?"

(In the past when a counselee asked for direct information like this, counselors were often taught to reframe the question in a way that put responsibility back on the counselee, like, "What do you think you should do?" While this has its place, Compass Therapy suggests that sometimes people need clear instructions about what to do next, especially when framed as strategies for personality growth that will ultimately help them solve inner conflicts).

"I think the first thing to do is cultivate this spirit of honesty that you've expressed here. The more you can talk openly about the spending and lying problem, the better, because it activates your Weakness compass point and helps you develop humility. Next, don't make sweeping promises of reform to Frank, since you may not be able to keep them until you've made greater progress. Instead, try something like, 'I'm working at being more up front about my spending, but I need to learn some new things along the way. It will help if you work with me gently and don't explode with anger if I blow it.' This combines Love with Assertion in that you're making a caring commitment to a course of change without promising the world."

Angela lets out a second sigh, this time of relief. "I can do that. He doesn't like getting angry with me. It's just that I've pushed him beyond all limits."

"Now tell me, Angela, when in the past do you first recall the Pleaser and Rule-breaker patterns working together in a way that pulled the wool over someone's eyes to get what you wanted?"

"It might have been in high school with my mother. I remember that I really wanted a new bracelet but didn't have enough money. She was taking a nap in her room and there were some bills on the dresser. I snuck in and slipped one off the bottom and it turned out to be a twenty-dollar bill—just what I needed. I was excited and scared at the same time, because when I bought the bracelet I knew I could never let her see it on me. So I wore it on dates but always took it off when I came home."

"Wow. I'm impressed with the ingenuity of your psyche to come up with such a solution. It made perfect sense to your unconscious, which knows nothing about rules and ethics, to get that bracelet no matter what, and wear it on special occasions. What was the down side?"

"That I quit feeling relaxed around Mom. It's like there was a secret wall between us that only I knew about. And I did repeat that act a couple more times."

"You stole from her?"

"I don't like that word."

"How else would you say it?"

"I borrowed her money thinking that someday I would pay her back."

"Did that day ever come?"

"No."

"Do you suppose this unconsciously affected the love between the two of you?"

(In this way you are stimulating Angela to think in new ways about her motivation and behavior, both past and present).

"I suppose I developed a reserve around her. I think I was dreading the day she'd put everything together and accuse me of stealing. I couldn't stand the thought of being mortified. So I played the part of the perfect daughter without feeling any love."

"So in your early attempts to solve this issue of buying something you wanted while deceiving someone you loved, you opted for the excitement of spending and accepted the loss of loving. Does that sound accurate?"

Her eyes tear up. "I didn't realize all that was happening."

"Now here's an intriguing question for you. Have you repeated this pattern with Frank?"

She reflects for a few moments. "Now that you mention it, I feel around him exactly how I felt around my mother, that I should act the part of a perfect wife even though I'm ruining everything."

"Let's call what you've just said true remorse, the awareness that you feel sad about ruining something very precious to you—Frank's love."

You observe in Angela's body language that she is withdrawing to an interior place, a place where people often go in silence, a solitude where they seek to mend what is broken inside.

You wait respectfully for about a minute, and then say, "Angela, we've got to wind up for today. Can you put into words any discoveries you've made?"

She looks you in the eye. "I'm determined to put an end to this crazy pattern. It's not worth keeping. But I'm afraid of the next time it seems perfectly okay to spend too much and then hide it from Frank. How do I stop this?"

"The answer is gradual growth through genuine prayer and an earnest desire to develop your whole Self Compass in place of the Pleaser and Rule-breaker patterns. I suggest that you do the homework of positive growth steps offered in the chapters on both of these patterns in the book. Then let's continue next week with what you've learned."

(You don't shy away from assigning homework when someone wants to get new behavioral results, knowing how a one-hour counseling session per week often isn't enough to transform the other one-hundred-and-ten waking hours of living. So just like learning to write the alphabet in kindergarten or do algebra in middle school, homework helps the counselee concentrate on new material pertinent to transforming personality and relationships).

In Angela's case, by the fifth week she has coupled a compass understanding of her personality with growth stretches that establish more transparent communication with Frank. Because she has moved into the Weakness compass point and shared with him the previously secret history with her mother, they are now actively collaborating on helping her develop honesty in place of deceit, and Angela is confiding in Frank rather than isolating from him.

The paranoid Arguer and antisocial Rule-breaker patterns are admittedly difficult patterns to work with. The main thing is to stay centered in your professional identity, without having too great a need to fix the person. Sometimes growth is superficial and the person must return to life and rack up another round of misery before finding sufficient motivation to carry through with inner changes.

However, time and God are on your side, for the Holy Spirit, too, is working with this person's developmental history, ever seeking those breakthrough moments where honest confession is sustained long enough for insight and character maturation to develop. I like to think of this as moving toward redemptive hope. Whether it occurs in counseling and coaching, or in the course of a person's church and community life, it constitutes a miracle to behold.

14. WEAKNESS STUCK: WORRIER & LONER

Who among us doesn't feel weak and alone from time to time? But Weakness-stuck individuals feel weak and alone all the time. And worry or isolation functions as the norm for living.

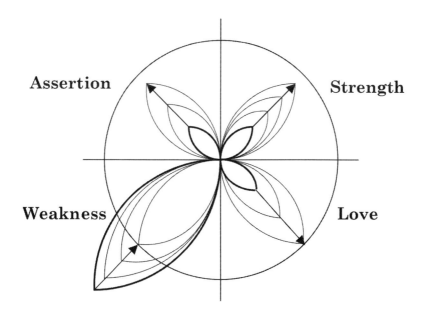

The Worrier and Loner Self Compass

As you can see from the compass diagram, the exaggerated Weakness compass point drains the life energy out of personality. The three other compass points of Love, Assertion, and Strength are placed on starvation rations, and the person as a whole becomes psychologically and spiritually anemic.

The result is to detach from others and withdraw from society. This negative strategy of saving the self by avoiding others is reinforced by a cycle of floundering or failures. School. Work. Marriage. Child-rearing. What occurs naturally for most people seems overwhelming to the Weakness-stuck person. And these unsuccessful experiences add up to the need to withdraw even further.

There are two primary ways people reveal that they are stuck on the Weakness compass point. In the *avoidant Worrier* pattern they care about what people think of them, yet feel helpless to make progress in life, worrying constantly about how badly they are coping. In the *schizoid Loner* pattern they actively distance from others, seeking safety in a hermit-like lifestyle.

By understanding these dynamics and knowing how to reverse them, pastoral counselors can slowly build a living dialogue that may well represent the counselee's first successful exchange of thoughts, feelings, and life energies with another person. Like a turtle that feels the warmth of the sun on its shell and begins to inch forward, so Worrier and Loner counselees can begin to discover the benefits of intimacy and community through the counseling bond. In so doing they experience a first heartwarming taste of human identity.

Weakness-Stuck Thoughts

Worrier: (For research, see Appendix, pp. 212-214).

  ⊕ I'd like to be accepted, but I know that people are out to ridicule me.

136

- No matter how hard I try, nothing works out. Sometimes I feel like just giving up.

- Dreams and fantasy are better than reality.

- No one is as scared and embarrassed as I am.

- I'm the last person to arrive and the first to leave.

- I can't stand disappointment.

Loner: (For research, see Appendix, pp. 214-216).

- I can do things better when people aren't around.

- I am a loner and an oddity.

- Relationships interfere with my freedom.

- People are replaceable objects.

- People should talk only when there's something to say.

- When people are out of sight, they are out of mind.

- I am safe when I am alone.

- I sometimes feel depressed about my boring life.

- Sometimes life is meaningless. I am nothing.

Worrier Counselees

I can identify with this pattern because in my seminary years I was haunted by it. I cared a great deal about Christ, and had even left medical school in response to God's call on my life. I read through the entire Bible several times, attended church weekly, and went to Campus Missions Fellowship on Friday nights. Yet I was still aware of a distance between me and other people. I couldn't put my finger on it, but it amounted to feeling lonely even when out with friends for pizza or having coffee at the student union. By the same token, I felt most comfortable when I was alone in my room cracking books, or researching a paper in the library stacks.

Most puzzling to me were the secret crying spells, the times I would withdraw to the prayer chapel late at night and cry. Why did I feel so alone? Why couldn't I interact as naturally as other people? The depression felt like a gunnysack of concrete on my chest, the hopelessness like a fist gripping my stomach.

I finally resolved to see a pastoral counselor at a nearby church, a very human man who seemed warm enough to entrust with my heart-wrenching worries.

Though my speech was halting and my melancholy palpable, I described what it was like to live within my secret cavern of loneliness.

He responded empathetically, but astutely. After asking a number of open-ended questions, he said, "Dan, I really feel for your pain. It seems to me that somewhere along your development you found human emotions too painful to handle, and that you created a rift between your mind and your heart. So your mind kept developing, and that's why you're so academically gifted, but your heart got left behind, and that's why you so feel so excluded from human community."

I felt my whole body relax. At last someone had found words for my deep dilemma, and that meant there might be a way out. In true avoidant Worrier fashion, I didn't go back to see him. Yet I never forgot his positive way of speaking about my condition, because it was obvious to me that he believed I could overcome the rift.

A few years later, when completing my doctoral work in counseling psychology, I got down to the business of personality growth that addressed what the pastoral counselor had diagnosed.

What put this problem behind me was realizing that I am an exceptionally sensitive person, just like many who become stuck on Weakness. As the pastoral counselor had suggested, I had incurred a lot of hurt and emotional woundedness in my growing up years and had unconsciously sought to resolve it through social withdrawal. Now with the help of some skilled counselors on the counseling faculty, I started replacing my negative self-image with cognitive and emotional skills for communicating with others.

One counselor put it this way: "Dan, you've got to shake the ghosts out of the trees and tell people how you feel. They can take it or leave it, but most of them will like you." This got my Strength compass point up and running. Another counselor gave me words of wisdom about Love: "Dan, you're constantly looking for a guarantee that someone will love you, when what you really need to do is take risks like everybody else." This got me exercising my Love compass point. And a professor gave me a priceless piece of guidance. "Dan, you're going to eventually die like we all do, so you might as well get on with living!" This awakened my Assertion.

It wasn't easy and it took months and years, but I did outgrow the trap of my former Weakness-stuck life. Yet I didn't leave the Weakness compass point behind, because in the course of building compass theory, I came to discover that it houses the root source of humility, a quality that Jesus ascribed to himself when he said, "Take my yoke upon you and learn from me, for I am gentle and humble in heart, and you will find rest for your souls" (Mt 11:29).

When you are counseling someone who manifests worry, you can discern rather quickly whether this worry is transitory, which usually responds well to brief situational coaching, or chronic and pervasive worry, which calls for insight and support through short-term counseling, or personality reconstruction in long-term pastoral psychotherapy.

When you encounter a chronic Worrier pattern, here are some insights you might offer: 1) Worry is a choice, not a necessity, although it often feels necessary to worry; 2) Worry actively distrusts God's involvement in life (most people never think of worry this way, but rather "sanctify" their worry as though it is a virtue); 3) Worry translated into action steps has redemptive value, but worry for worry's sake creates meaningless misery; and 4) Counselees can transfer the energy it takes to worry into prayer for guidance and positive steps for change.

At a physiological level, chronic worry may reflect the biochemical condition of major depression, a genetic disorder arising from the body's inability to produce enough catecholamine molecules in neuronal synapses. So it is a good idea as part of your professional support system to meet with a psychiatrist or family doctor who is acquainted with major depression, and who can act as a medical referral for counselees whose symptoms seem unabated by psychological and spiritual counseling strategies.

In this case, you can say to your counselee: "I have a hunch that a portion of your pattern of worry and withdrawal is biological. I suggest that you see Dr. _____ and explain your symptoms, because taking an appropriate antidepressant is like receiving a prescription for eyeglasses: it helps the world come into better focus so that you can feel more confident in facing life."

If the counselee follows through and receives a prescription, you continue right along with the pastoral counseling and coaching, helping them integrate the effects of the meds with their personality and relationship development.

By way of an overall counseling strategy, keep before you the Compass Model, so that at times you can guide the counselee's attention to growth steps in Assertion, and other times developing Strength or Love. By the same token, you don't push too hard, because you respect the secret security these counselees draw from the Weakness compass point, since as long as they stay there they don't have to take risks or assume responsibility. So you relax, even when they express uncertainty, self-doubt, and fear, and in so doing, you create an interpersonal atmosphere that de-catastrophizes their worry, offering your calmness to counter their anxiety (Strength), your practical suggestions to counter their learned helplessness (Assertion), and your faithful caring to counter their depersonalization (Love).

You don't take on the unrealistic project of turning them into industrious and confident persons, but rather assist them through either an extended course of counseling, or occasional meetings, to construct a developmental bridge that helps them move from fear-filled existence to a more abundant life. In a pastoral context, you can pray that they receive the spiritual empowerment of fortitude. At the end of a session, will courage to them by affirming their gradual progress and conveying warm encouragement.

Loner Counselees

The Loner lifestyle usually stems from negative experiences that interrupt psychosocial development. The person tries to survive by withdrawing from relationships, sometimes intensified by a biogenetic tendency to withdraw as well. You work to uncover the hidden woundedness and how it was generalized into arrested growth. Then you weave back and forth from those recollections to current life events, showing Loners how they are now free to utilize the compass points of Love, Strength, and Assertion to spring them free from habitual reliance upon Weakness.

Some Loners are actually aware and proud of a hermit-like existence, and in this case you face a fascinating opportunity for Christian discipleship, in that such counselees have never internalized the full calling of Christ on their life.

Loners can attend church while actually keeping the Lord at arm's length, deliberately not surrendering their personality and destiny to him because their habitual aloofness prevents a heartwarming encounter. In pastoral counseling, they may come to see the Lord in a new light, through the humanity of the pastoral counselor, augmented by the Holy Spirit, that invites a mutual dialogue.

Usually a Loner comes into counseling through the discontent of a spouse, who likely feels disheartened in trying to elicit an emotional, cognitive, or spiritual response from their mate. Perhaps as a consequence of socialization, most incommunicado spouses are men. In middle school and high school, boys train one another to keep their tender feelings to themselves, repressing their needs for emotional nurturance in order to act strong and independent, yet mute about their real emotions—except for anger, which is considered a show of masculinity.

When a wife, whether as a young bride or longstanding partner, expects more than caricatures of communication, the Loner sees her desire for intimacy as a source of irritation, her pleas for emotional and conversational connection falling on deaf ears.

I have had hundreds of initial phone calls from women seeking marriage counseling who end their query by saying, "But my husband doesn't think we have a problem, and when we had counseling once before, he didn't say much."

Yet such men can experience growth gains when you actively engage them during sessions, especially when you amplify whatever they say and compliment them on saying anything at all. They will feel relieved that they are not going to be humiliated, and actually build confidence that they can say a few things that really count. It is wise to use compass terms early on; otherwise, the sheer inertia of the Loner's non-participation can arrest progress and cause the individual or the couple to abandon the counseling process. Though progress is slow and arduous, it does come.

Picture this couple's first session. Muriel bursts forth with a litany of complaints about how frustrated she feels making so many decisions without Harry's input, and how she gets so tired of his one-word responses. You notice how walled-off he looks, and say, "So Harry, can you tell me why you don't talk to Muriel more?"

"I talk to her plenty," he mutters. "I say 'yes' when I mean yes and 'no' when I mean no. You don't need any more words than that."

"He's always been this way," Muriel wails. "He ignores me except when I drag something out of him."

You know that this couple needs time for Muriel to ventilate her anguish and for you to establish some kind of rapport with Harry. So you spend most of the session gathering information and exploring what situations cause the most meltdowns. Then you say, "Next session I'm going to introduce you both to the Self Compass. But my impressions for now are that Muriel uses the Controller pattern to try to get conversations going, and that you, Harry, use the Loner pattern to get her off your case. Does that ring any bells?"

Muriel says, "I do try to control him because if I didn't we wouldn't have a marriage."

Harry shrugs. "I think it's all her problem."

In the second session, after explaining how the Self Compass works, you say to Harry, "When did you first come to believe that keeping everything to yourself was the best way through life?"

(You are shuttling between the counselee's past and present. All personality patterns originate through a combination of genetic temperament factors interacting with an emerging selfhood that seeks to cope with environmental stressors. Past behavior carries into the present without awareness that a truncated Self Compass is blocking behavioral options. By following Harry's consciousness into his past history, you open a channel of communication that may entice him to understand and alter his present behavior).

"Army basic training. I was eighteen."

"What was it like?"

143

"Hell—worst place on earth. Hated it."

"How come?"

"Nobody wanted to be there. Terrible things happened. I don't want to think about it."

"What did you learn?"

"Keep your mouth shut. Keep your nose out of people's business."

"And did this become your life philosophy?"

"You bet."

(You turn to Muriel for a maneuver in marriage counseling that is crucial for moving forward; that is, interpreting what one partner is saying in new words that the other partner can understand).

"Muriel," you say, "I think Harry just told us a great deal about himself. Here he was a young man in a social situation that felt like prison, where men were unspeakably cruel to each other because everyone hated being there. He had to survive without anyone helping him. And he formed a brilliant solution that kept him alive and out of trouble: 'Keep everything to yourself.'"

Harry nods almost imperceptibly, and because you are astute at noting any changes in a counselee's eyes, you see the microsecond in which moisture flashes across his eyes, even though his accustomed habit of repressing feelings quickly cuts off any tears.

Muriel turns to Harry and says accusingly, "You never told me that story!"

You raise your hand slightly to get her attention, and then say, "Muriel, I don't know if you're aware of it or not, but Harry just bared his soul to us, and you've responded with a sharp criticism."

Muriel winces. "I'm sorry. I was just so surprised. I wish he'd talk to me like this more often."

(Now you start making tie-ins between compass theory and human behavior, confident to do this because counselees are unconsciously hungry for meaning in their lives).

"So, Harry, you learned through this formative military experience to keep everything to yourself, right?"

"Yep."

"Here's what I think may have happened when you two got married. Muriel was in love with you and excited about sharing life and communication on many levels. And you were in love with her, Harry, except that you carried into the marriage your Loner philosophy of 'Keep everything to yourself.' This set up a one-sided communication style that was doomed to frustration—Muriel pursuing and pursuing, you avoiding and avoiding. How does that sound?"

"It's true enough, but there's nothing I can do about it," says Harry. "What's done is done."

"Now I wonder if that philosophy is starting to kick in right here in our session," you say. "Like, 'If I quit talking about it, it will go away.'"

Harry shrugs. "I told her we don't need counseling."

(Because you won't allow yourself to be stumped by disjointed communications, you continue to build rapport and press forward, at least enough so that this couple will have something new to think about if they choose to show up again).

"Well, that is up to the two of you. But I want to ask you one question, Harry. Do you love Muriel?"

"Sure," he says. "I've always loved her. But that doesn't mean I have to be a chatterbox."

"Yet I want to suggest that while the army philosophy of life worked great in the army, it isn't well-suited for married love. In fact, clamming up for too many years can destroy the love between you."

Muriel dabs her eyes with a Kleenex. Harry looks visibly moved by her pain. "Muriel," you say, "can you tell us two ways Harry can show love to you without a lot of talking?"

"Well," she says tentatively, softly, "if he'd hold my hand when we're out walking, and if he'd tell me more about what he wants or doesn't want, that would help."

"What do you think, Harry?" you say. "A possibility?"

"I don't see what holding hands has to do with it, but I'll give it a try." He reaches over and grabs her hand.

"Excellent. And offering her a little more information about your preferences?"

"That's harder. I just don't care about a lot of things. That's why I don't say anything."

"But you care a lot about golfing," says Muriel. "And you put a lot of energy into how your game goes."

Not wanting the session to deteriorate into mutual accusations, you offer an interpretation to Harry regarding what Muriel just said. "Harry, I think Muriel is saying that she wants a human response from you, and that when you're mute around her, or when you put emotional excitement into golf balls instead of her, she feels left out. Do you suppose you might give this some thought?"

"Yep."

"The good news, Harry," you continue, "is that you're a man who speaks plainly, so we're always going to know where you stand."

"You can count on that. If I have an opinion I'll tell you what it is. If I don't, I won't."

"That's a solid start," you say, "and I predict if you two keep coming back, you're going to become very skilled at showing Muriel your love."

He grins sheepishly. "That'll be the day."

"Yes," you say, smiling at them both. "With God's help, it will."

15. STRENGTH STUCK: BOASTER & CONTROLLER

Stuck with too much Strength, *narcissistic Boasters* and *compulsive Controllers* relate to others on a one-way street that establishes power over people through a superiority that paradoxically wipes out prospects for psychological and spiritual intimacy.

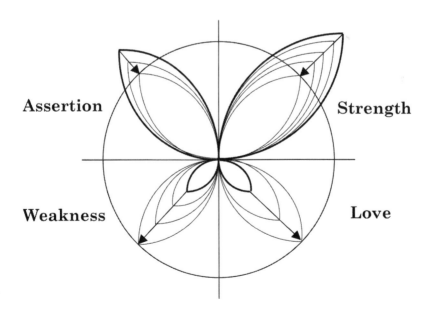

The Boaster and Controller Self Compass

Notice how the exaggerated Strength compass point compensates for shrunken Weakness and Love compass points. This is because the person is unwilling to experience the emotional vulnerability required for both humility and love. Instead, the person wants guarantees that remove all uncertainty from life, which leads to their need to see themselves as superior to or controlling of other people. The fact that the Assertion compass point is also exaggerated means they will insist on how right they are and become testy if anyone disagrees.

Boasters and Controllers differ in that while Boasters simply assume their grandiosity (perhaps because of looks, money, or having been spoiled as a child), Controllers actually put in the time and effort, working tirelessly to demonstrate how efficient and capable they are.

However, there is a fly in the ointment. People can repress the Weakness compass point, but they can't get rid of it. So the harder Strength-stuck individuals strive to prove their flawlessness, the more others see their clay feet and recognize how self-absorbed and condescending they are.

There is another quality that they exude: joy-killing. Boasters don't like hearing about other people's successes or accomplishments because it makes them feel threatened, so they brag all the more about their achievements or future plans. Controllers likewise are joy-killers, but for a different reason. They are joyless individuals whose minds are always processing items on to-do lists or noticing what someone else hasn't done perfectly, so they spend a considerable amount of energy criticizing others "to try to make them better." A spouse, child, or co-worker of a Controller learns that nothing is ever good enough.

Strength-stuck individuals objectively know the people around them, but don't subjectively enjoy them. Others exist as objects to serve one's ego needs, not as persons in their own right. This means that an unconscious superiority complex undercuts the capability to love others and God.

Loving requires humility about one's weaknesses, patience with other's mistakes, and delight in the overall humanness of the other person. But Strength-stuck individuals short-circuit this process by hiding their weakness under the mantle of compensatory strength, being impatient with others, and rejecting of their feelings and needs. Though they certainly engage people, an overblown self-sufficiency leaves them inwardly very alone.

Strength-Stuck Thoughts:

Boaster: (For research, see Appendix, pp. 216-218).

⊕ If I am powerful enough, I can be totally confident and eliminate all self-doubt.

⊕ I am superior to others and they should grant me special privileges.

⊕ I am above the rules. I can do whatever I wish to reinforce my superior status and to expand my aura of influence.

⊕ I am entitled to admiration and people should feel grateful to have me around.

⊕ If you love me, you'll do whatever I want, when I want.

⊕ I have no use for people who don't hold me in high regard.

⊕ I don't like it when someone else in a group gets special attention.

⊕ All that matters is what I want, feel, or think.

- Very few people are worth my time; the rest bore me.

- I must succeed in order to prove my superiority.

- You are present in my life to admire me.

Controller: (For research, see Appendix, pp. 218-220).

- I must always be in control and do everything right the first time.

- People should do things my way.

- Thinking is always superior to feeling.

- There's a correct solution for all problems.

- You ought never throw anything away because you might need it later (Steketee & Frost, 2003).

- You should organize each day with a to-do list that must be completed before bedtime.

- To make a mistake is to deserve criticism.

- You can keep yourself from making a mistake by always being careful and thorough.

- People should do better and try harder and never shrink from duty.

- I have to enforce high standards on others because otherwise they will fall short.

- Enforcing rules is the best way through life.

⊕ Criticizing people helps them avoid future mis-
    takes.

Boaster Counselees

While Boasters will not be aware of their own narcissism,
you will quickly recognize it. The presentation of the problem and the life history narrative will amply attest that they
view themselves in an exaggeratedly positive light, endowed
with gifts that make them special.

Nor should you resist this impression. In fact, the best
way to proceed is to resonate with their claim to fame, giving
them the accolades they are seeking.

Why?

Underneath the cool exterior exists a fragile sense of self.
The very ego defense mechanisms they use the most—denial
of deficiency, repression of blind spots, exaltation of the
self—are built on shaky ground. There may be a reference to
their high IQ, or their absolute success in the business
world, or their total charm with the opposite sex, but ultimately most of these claims are more make believe than
real, reflecting the need to live in a universe where they are
admired and lauded.

The truth is that most Boasters are unwilling to put in
disciplined hours for genuine mastery and are accustomed to
receiving the glory in advance of the effort, as though they
are saying, "The real truth is that I am the greatest because
if I ever really applied myself I'd naturally rise to the top."

So you hear and echo all the good stuff, and wait pa-
tiently for the bad stuff—those little peeps of partial admis-
sion where they halfway own a very real weakness. Then
you proceed with care and the compass model to reframe the
acknowledgment of weakness as a great strength and the
over-exaggeration of strength as a potential weakness.

Julio has come back to you for a second session, and con-
fesses that he saw himself as a Boaster in *The Self Compass*
book.

"It was a pretty big shock to see myself there," he says, "because I always think of myself as helping other people, like that's why my car dealership is the best in the state, because I give people what they want."

"So what was so shocking about the Boaster pattern?"

"It says that I'm totally selfish, that I'm out for number one, that I use people to get what I want out of life."

"And that contradicts your self-image?"

"Of course it does. I'm not the devil!"

"So how does this bear on your goals for counseling?"

"Well, it doesn't have so much to do with what I came in for—the anxiety that wakes me up at night. But it has to do with something a little more personal. Something I'm not exactly proud to mention."

"Go ahead. It's safe here."

"It's my lust."

"What about it?"

"It's there all the time. Even when I'm selling cars to women, I'm hoping they'll bend over and give me a good view."

"And has this been with you for long?"

"Since I was a little boy I was fascinated with girls. I would get aroused playing with them on the school swings. In middle school I fantasized about how the women teachers would look with no clothes on. And then in college I really went off the deep end."

(You stay relaxed, knowing that in pastoral counseling people can say the unsayable, and in doing so they open whole new avenues for self-understanding and actualizing growth. You are listening to Julio with one ear attuned to his unfolding story, and the other attuned to how and when a compass interpretation can bring everything into better focus. You also take care to reflect what he is telling you in a positive enough light that he'll continue).

"So you grew up being a keen appreciator of sensuality and the sexual dimension of girls and women."

"Exactly. A real connoisseur of sex. In college I became a babe magnet. Maybe it was my looks or how smart I am but girls practically stood in line."

"You sound very proud of this history."

Julio smiles. "What can I say? I'm a born lover."

"So what is the problem in all of this?"

(This surprise response lets Julio know you are not doing counseling to become his moral judge, and that if he doesn't want to bring an issue forward, you aren't going to do it for him).

"The problem is that I'm married and I can't keep my eyes off other women. Veronica catches me in restaurants or grocery stores looking at women's rear ends. I used to deny it and tell her that she was paranoid, but it's happened so much that I can't get away with that anymore."

You take a deep breath and offer an empathetic look. "I really feel for you, Julio. Lust is a very powerful force in personality and it seems like it has invaded your married life to the point of creating deep pain in Veronica."

"It's awful to see how hurt she is. I've promised to reform many times, but then later I forget all about it and it happens again when I don't expect it."

"Julio, tell me honestly. What is your level of motivation for making progress in diminishing your lust toward other women and increasing your love and fidelity toward Veronica?"

(This is a legitimate question, because with deeper commitment on his part to make progress, you gain more permission for coaching him about his personality pattern).

"I really want to solve this. It's threatening us big time."

"Okay. Let's talk about the Boaster pattern, because this pattern in your personality is going to try and talk you out of any progress."

"What do you mean?"

"The Boaster pattern you adopted early in life gave you the illusion that you could have your cake and eat it, too—

that you could enjoy the excitement of lust without bothering to learn how to communicate with a woman. The string of women conquests in college seemed to prove the point. Just tell a woman what she wants to hear and then get her in the sack. Is that accurate?"

"That's how it worked."

"Now what was it that made you move from woman to woman, insatiable?"

"I'd get bored as soon as the chase was over. Just when the girl would think she had me, I'd dump her."

"So even though you looked like a ladies man who had a following like a harem, in fact you were a narcissist who wanted nothing to do with communication, other than sweet-talking them into bed."

(It's okay to say things this clearly, if there is no moralistic "shoulding" transmitted through your tone of voice or body language. Counselees do want to hear an expert opinion on their issues, and part of the value of talking to you is removing the smoke and mirror distortions that their patterns create).

"I don't like seeing myself that way, but I'm sure that's what it amounted to."

"You are being very courageous right now, and I compliment your willingness to speak so frankly. Now here's the important thing about the Boaster pattern: it depersonalizes relationships because it gives you the illusion that surface communication is all you need, even in marriage. The pattern prohibits deeper emotions like vulnerability or uncertainty, yet these are required for a loving relationship."

"Uh-oh. You just said a bad word."

"What was that?"

"Vulnerability. I hate that word. Something in me wants to avoid it like the plague."

"What does it mean to you?"

"That someone will have power over me. That they won't admire me anymore. That I'm going to be hurt."

"Like Veronica has been hurt by your Boaster pattern?"

(This quick interpretation encourages a moment of discovery and empathy by likening the hurt he avoids with the hurt Veronica has received).

"Yeah. Like I've hurt Veronica. Damn. It's the last thing I wanted to do."

"Yet the Boaster pattern predicts that you would become an emotionally unavailable partner who could not develop a faithful love, and would inevitably hurt your partner by needing sexual energy from other women."

(Now you sense that you've gone far enough for one session in making Julio aware of the pattern that has run his life for years. Your intuition says that if you go a step further, he may suddenly bolt and become too self-conscious, feeling that you don't like or accept him. So now you switch gears to build him up and assure him of your respect so that he can leave the session with a degree of dignity).

"This is a new way to look at it all," says Julio.

"I think we've covered some good territory today, and I commend you for your openness."

Julio looks relieved. "So what do I tell Veronica when she asks me what we talked about?"

"Tell her these sessions are confidential, but that you're getting some insight into yourself. Would you like me to pray a prayer of blessing for you?"

"Please do."

"Dear Lord," you say, "thank you for bringing this sensitive subject to Julio's attention. Please begin a healing work in him that extends to Veronica, that they might have their marriage repaired, and that Julio might integrate sexuality with personality in a way that serves them both. Amen."

"Thank you," says Julio, clearing his throat. "I haven't ever prayed about this because I felt too embarrassed."

"You've done an excellent job today of being open to our communication. I don't recommend that you do anything special this week, other than becoming aware that you really want a good marriage with lots of love, and you're going to take the needed steps to make this possible."

(This reflects sensitivity on your part that growth in difficult areas—like the transformation of lust into love and communication—happens gradually, requiring the counselee to assimilate new concepts and principles that make sense and can slowly turn the tide. You especially avoid the trap of being too heavy-handed, like saying, "Lust is an evil you should avoid at all cost," or "You just need more willpower to resist lustful urges," because the Boaster pattern will likely sabotage this moral mandate, and the counselee, feeling shamed and condemned, may cancel the next session. A further principle of Compass Therapy recommends that you do not try to remove a negative trait from someone's life by just focusing on that trait. In this case, focusing too much on lust would only magnify the problem and intensify the feeling of failure. But by expanding the focus to include a larger portion of life and personality, you can end up developing the very dimensions that through their prior absence contributed to out-of-control lust. Gradually, then, with actualizing growth in this larger domain, the presenting problem loses its power to dominate and its energies are transformed into a richer personality).

By the fourth session, Julio is becoming more adept at integrating his Strength and Weakness compass points, making fewer boastful statements and more honest assessments of his progress and failures. He is inviting Veronica out on dates and really listening to what she has to say, building upon your role-playing with Julio about how to hear and reflect someone's feelings. He takes in your ideas for how to carry on lovemaking with Veronica instead of merely having sex. The fact that you compliment him for the slightest success in these areas is bolstering his risk-taking and willingness to keep learning.

In a sixth session Julio reports that Veronica is becoming a more fun sexual partner.

"So it's like Veronica is opening up to you sexually because she feels prized by you emotionally. Is that right?"

"It's the most amazing thing. Our sex life used to be so boring because I was always pushing for something new that she didn't want to do. But now that I know how to build her up, she's really quite adventurous."

"What is happening on the lust front with other women?"

"That's still there, but less than it used to be. I think I'm realizing that an orgasm is just an orgasm, and that love is what makes it special. And since I'm feeling more of that with Veronica, there's less lust floating around inside me."

"This is wonderful news, Julio. It sounds like you have a good handle on what originally brought you to counseling."

"That's what I was going to say today. I think I'm ready to take it from here."

"Why don't we go ahead and make this the stopping point. And remember, you're welcome back anytime."

Controller Counselees

Controller-patterned counselees take counseling very seriously, and if you don't come across as knowledgeable and confident, they can lose respect for you in a hurry. Also, you must activate your own compass rhythm of firmness and flexibility or they will turn an issue into a power struggle.

Frances comes to you at the suggestion of the senior pastor who has just experienced a battle of the wills with her and offered pastoral counseling as a possible resource for expressing her dismay and discontent.

This is a context in which you take particular care in what you say and do. On the one hand, you want to establish a boundary of confidentiality whereby you never mention Frances or anything she shares with the senior pastor who is your colleague on the pastoral staff, and on the other hand you want to give Frances your best guidance without becoming part of the ax she is grinding in the church.

In a first session Frances gets down to business. "As you know, Martin and I have been attending this church for three months, which is a concession I made to his liturgical background as a Christian. But I've about had it with how this church handles communion, and I told the pastor as much last Sunday. I have no idea why he suggested pastoral counseling with you, but here I am!"

"My goodness, it seems that something about this church's tradition has struck you really wrong, and now you feel shuffled off to me and can't figure out why."

"That's right. Now do you want to know about the incident or should I tell you more about me?"

(This concern with "proper procedure" is an early warning sign that raises in your mind the prospect of the Controller pattern in full form).

"I'd like you to go with what seems most urgent right now."

"All right then. I've told my husband for years that real wine should not be served in communion because it is a bad example to youth and it can trigger alcoholic cravings in any adults who are alcoholic. But he just says I am narrow-minded. I am tired of being pooh-poohed. There are plenty of churches that serve grape juice and everybody knows it stands for the blood of Christ, but nobody gets tempted by the taste or smell of liquor."

"And so did you feel it was your moral duty to inform the pastor of this?"

(You are filling in the blanks of the compulsive Controller pattern and in so doing signaling not only empathy with Frances, but also knowledge of how her mind processes data about life).

"Absolutely. I also told him that the bread part of communion would be more realistic if he used real loaves of bread instead of prefabricated wafers, which aren't anything at all like what Jesus really used in the Lord's Supper."

"And how did he respond?"

"With a completely closed mind, like he knew all the answers and I knew nothing, even though I've researched this topic and have come to my opinion with a great deal of thought. I'm purely concerned with the quality of worship that the congregation experiences on Sundays, and when I see a glaring mistake that needs correcting, I can't help but feel that the Lord is guiding me to bring it to the pastor's attention."

"I'm just curious, but have you ever found a church where you felt they did everything right?"

"I'm glad you brought that up because I don't want to appear judgmental or small-minded, but in my opinion most churches don't come close to what the original church experienced. There is a moral laxity that is best illustrated by Christ's chastisement of many churches in the book of Revelation."

"So your study of church history and your keen sense of what's right and wrong in bringing people to Christ makes you a staunch advocate of how churches in general, and this church in particular, should function."

"Exactly." Frances smiles and breathes more easily. "Now don't get me wrong. I'm not asking for complete perfection. But I am concerned about the things that can be fixed and made better."

(Once you've gathered basic information and built a workable rapport, you move in directions that may be new to Frances, but hold promise in helping her eventually solve the confrontations that she unknowingly perpetuates).

"Tell me, Frances, about what you enjoy in life."

She sits back in her seat. "Well, I enjoy being the troop leader of Girl Scouts in this region. It's a very demanding job but I have good organizational skills and provide lots of activities that I think young girls should engage in if they are to become responsible citizens in the community."

"I appreciate how you give of yourself to enrich the lives of the new generation. And how is the job going?"

Frances shrugs. "If I could only keep the Scout leaders on the ball, I'd be a lot happier. I do such a conscientious job of scheduling campouts, museum trips, and cultural events, but some group leader always manages to get something wrong and ruin a perfect outing."

"And how do you handle that?"

"I bring it to their attention. I'm not here to play babysitter. Raising young girls properly is a very serious endeavor. I learned a long time ago that doing the right thing doesn't win you a popularity contest, but it does give the sense of a job well done."

"Let me ask you a question. Aside from the run-in with the pastor, would you like to reduce the stress in your life?"

"Ha! As if living wasn't all about managing stress. Stress goes with the territory of leadership and responsibility. I'm not about to shirk my duties because of a little stress."

At this moment you might start feeling hemmed in, as though Frances is an impregnable fortress whom you wish would transfer membership to another church.

But then you recall how in Compass Therapy, the secret of personality growth and therapeutic progress often lies in the dynamic between polarities. Your unconscious supplies your conscious mind with these interconnected insights and principles: 1) A counselee's presenting or public self represents their most conscious way of relating to the world—in Frances' case, as a morally righteous, upstanding person who, from her view, only judges others because they need correcting; 2) Persons overly leveraged into Strength possess an equally strong unconscious dimension to their behavior, a dimension that they neither recognize nor understand—in Frances' case, her Weakness compass point; and 3) You can often make headway with the Controller pattern by describing the repressed components of the counselee's personality, because this will strike a chord of truth within them, a kind of "A-ha" experience of finally integrating parts of the self that were formerly unconscious.

You don't go too far in this. A counselee might not be ready for much transformation in a particular session or episodic visit to a counselor, but they may become more open a few months or a year later. So if all Frances wants from this session is to feel justified in setting the pastor straight about communion practices by vindicating herself to you, then you will conclude the session with no further agreed-upon goals, and terminate the counseling. But if she responds to the feelers you put out, designed to awaken her unconscious, then she will feel motivated to set up a next session.

So you say, "Well, I believe you are a person with strong values and a commitment to excellence in all that you undertake. I'm just wondering if you ever feel lonely inside."

For the first time, Frances doesn't have an automatic pilot comeback. She tilts her head in thought, but then sets her mouth into a stiff upper lip and says, "Oh, sure, doesn't everybody?" But the normally confident tone is gone.

"I suppose so, but I'm wondering if this burden of always being right doesn't somehow isolate you, doesn't leave you feeling guilty sometimes, because you're not quite perfect?"

"I do feel guilty when I'm not performing up to my true potential. That's the cross I bear."

"And do you share it with anyone?"

"Heavens, no. One mustn't be a worrywart or sourpuss."

"Do you share it with the Lord?"

Frances looks taken aback. "After all that Christ went through to redeem me on the cross? I'm going to complain to him about feeling bad? I think not. What are you getting at, anyway?"

"I'm working on a hypothesis in compass theory, a principle which suggests that people who carry extra heavy loads of duty and responsibility sometimes haven't discovered how to relax and enjoy the grace of God."

"What do you mean?"

"I mean that being too strong can put you out of touch with your weakness, where you become your own worst critic, and drive yourself to distraction with a 'tyranny of the shoulds.'"

For the first time, the session falls silent. You relax in your chair, breathing deeply, knowing that a counselee needs to inwardly reflect on new ideas that have not occurred to them before. You also know that you have broached the hallowed ground of the unconscious, a place where even Frances is uninformed. She may feel thunder struck before a numinous concept she's on the verge of grasping—that a significant proportion of her life energy is sapped by the Tyrant whose name is Perfection.

Or she may be getting ready to gather up her purse and bid you adieu.

Christ knew many moments like this, when he spoke the truth in love and waited to see if individuals would seek more or beat a hasty exit.

Frances looks at you, and you see a trace of moisture in her eyes. Her voice is softer when she speaks. "I've never had anybody put it like that. But I do feel under quite a lot of pressure. And sometimes I do feel all alone."

"Frances, I take my hat off to you for your open mind. If I'm on the right track, you may be living under the gun of the Controller pattern, a style of personality that specializes in setting such high standards for behavior that neither you nor anyone else can achieve them."

"But I try so hard. Doesn't that count for anything?"

"If I can interpret what you just said, that's the Controller pattern at work, telling you that needing some personality growth implies you're a total failure. In other words, if you're not absolutely perfect, then you are completely worthless."

Frances' shoulders relax and drop about half an inch. "Why does it feel good to hear you say that? That I'm okay without being perfect."

"Because it's true. Your unconscious has been waiting for the day that you could relax enough to see what's stacked up inside you. To unpack the secret stress, tension, guilt—and fear of being judged and found wanting. And counseling is a safe place for doing that. If you'd like to continue next week, we can look into what programmed you toward perfectionism early on, and what you can do about it."

"I'd like that."

PART IV: PASTORAL CARE

16. THE PASTORAL COUNSELOR'S SELF COMPASS

The Self Compass growth tool edifies a pastoral counselor's life and personality as effectively as it does a counselee's.

After becoming a psychologist, I unknowingly developed a glitch in my personality. I was so self-confident (Strength compass point) that I lacked humility and empathy toward my counselees (Weakness compass point). In other words, I had plenty of clinical skills as a therapist, but lacked the ability to identify with a counselee's vulnerabilities. I wasn't about to feel vulnerable, especially because I had spent too much time there in my growing up years.

Looking back on that early part of my counseling career, I recognize that God was trying to wake me up, trying to give me clues that being too strong had become my greatest weakness, but I didn't want to hear the message. Though I utilized healthy strength in accomplishing goals, a residue of the Boaster pattern kept me self-absorbed and one step removed from other people's pain—too success-oriented to empathize with others.

Several things happened that brought a compass awakening. There was an extended period of illness, a devastating financial reversal, and the death of my father. After taking off several months from counseling in order to put my life back together, the first few counselees I took into a renewed practice commented that they especially appreciated my empathy.

What? Empathy? From the Rock of Gibraltar who felt superior to almost everyone? Yet as I reflected on this new input, I had to agree that it was true. Somehow in the crucible of my suffering, God had balanced out my over-reliance upon Strength, helping me to develop a more authentic integration of healthy Weakness.

Now I found myself tearing up when someone experienced a broken heart or inconsolable loss. I also found myself laughing with them in their joy or comforting them in their loneliness. I came to realize that I no longer feared feeling temporarily weak, or coming across as a real person. It's like I could now see in my mind's eye the Self Compass in the course of every day, and accept that I, Dan Montgomery, was a good enough human being, with strengths and weaknesses taken together.

I don't know what your particular insights will be as we explore the Self Compass in the pastoral counselor's personality, but I want you to know that I am with you in support of your discoveries.

The Rhythm of Love and Assertion

Most people I've met who have gone into counseling as a vocation say they did so because they cared about others. They wanted to help heal persons who were hurting. Yet there is a paradox in counseling, in that counselees can resist a counselor's assistance as much as they receive it. This means you can't maintain a naïve belief that loving counselees is enough to make them whole.

In fact, loving care can get you in a lot of trouble if you cross certain boundaries with the counselee, developing too much interpersonal intimacy. Many counselors undergo the inglorious experience of falling in love with one of their counselees. This doesn't mean that the counselor acts on this sentiment, because it is equally feasible that the counselor will recognize the inappropriateness of deepening a misguided love bond, and will confide in a supervisor or else do the inner work of intercepting the subjective side of love, transmuting it back into objective caring by not giving it room to grow.

It is wise to understand that the counseling platform allows for such profound communion of souls that transparency can succumb to infatuation, where professional caring takes a headlong fall into the ditch of a love affair. In the years before having sex with counselees became public knowledge as a glaring legal and professional breach of ethics, counselors sometimes took such liberties. Now, however, it is at the top of everyone's list—counselors and counselees alike—to channel caring into facilitating the growth and coping skills of the counselee without becoming enmeshed in a romantic/erotic mess.

It is erroneous to think that pastoral counselors, because of their consecration to God and assimilation of Christian doctrine, are immune from such temptations, for they certainly are not. Yet that immunity is available, and it comes through the awareness that the Love compass point needs effective balancing with the Assertion compass point in the pastoral counselor's life and practice.

What the Love compass points enables you to do is forgive counselees for the mistakes, broken resolutions, and sometimes glaringly immature attitudes they will reveal to you, while nurturing them with a long-term sustenance much akin to Christ's love for his disciples.

Assertion, on the other hand, lets you stand apart from the counselee, holding your own as a person in your own right, so as not to become drawn into the counselee's habitual way of relating to people. For if a counselee can draw you into their normal interpersonal style and get you to agree with their perspective, then you will completely lose your power to effect constructive change in their life. Put differently, you give up the need for your counselee's approval and gain the ability to tell them the actual effects of their distorted personality patterns, truncated human nature, and self-defeating communication style.

Assertion lets you express yourself in ways that include professional knowledge you've acquired from study, training, and experience. Assertion lets you make tentative hypotheses about a counselee's unconscious dynamics, even though such information is often startling at first, or runs counter to their conscious self-image. Of course, you don't allow your assertion to become headstrong or brash, because the balance of the Love compass point is there to reign you in, reminding you that love is patient, kind, and not rude or arrogant.

Think about this polarity for a moment. Picture the ways you show the Love compass point in your personal and professional life: caring, forgiving, nurturing, supporting. Now move to the opposite compass point and picture the ways you manifest Assertion: expressing, diplomatically confronting, negotiating, and challenging. Now let the two polarities move into a dynamic rhythm that encompasses many shades and nuances of love and assertion, working synergistically to give your personality and interpersonal communication a balance of loving assertion and assertive loving. It is reassuring to know that if you become too loving, sliding into subjective caring that becomes inappropriate, you can recover quickly by moving into assertion and making choices that restore balance. Or if you stay too long in assertion to the point of argumentativeness, contrariness, or unforgiveness, you can recover your balance by moving into love.

The key to this attitudinal and behavioral flexibility lies in existential openness to God's guidance. Just as the disciples needed open minds and flexible personalities in order to keep hearing and benefiting from Jesus' interactions with them, so the Holy Spirit can spontaneously move within your personality and behavior, both in counseling sessions and in your private life. And your ability to guide counselees toward Christlike wholeness radiates from your own continued growth in Christ.

The Rhythm of Weakness and Strength

In terms of the Weakness and Strength polarity within your personality, there is a profound bit of wisdom conveyed through Scripture but often lost in culture at large.

The entry point for following Christ comes through weakness, not strength. Compass Therapy purposely uses the term "Weakness" to highlight the universality of human fallibility—conjoined with the truth that acknowledging one's weaknesses leads to humility and empathy for others.

If you think about it, no one in the biblical narrative called upon God or followed Christ out of sheer human strength. Such strength creates the sense that one is fully capable of living one's life without God's help. But biblical characters, to the degree that they developed intimacy with God, uniformly confessed their weaknesses and acknowledged their sin and need.

As a pastoral counselor, you build upon this willingness to acknowledge your humanness and resist appearing infallible. In your personal and professional life, you maintain an ongoing dialogue with the Lord, based on your need for him to impart to you some of his own qualities as the Mighty Counselor. Yet even Christ lives out this polarity of Weakness and Strength. As the author of Hebrews points out, he makes perfect intercession for his brother and sister humans, since he himself has suffered and knows what it's like to be human.

There are going to be times when you leave a particular counseling session feeling quite furious at the counselee for dumping anger on you, or for ignoring your advice and worsening their situation. You'll want to tell God, "Bill is a total idiot! Why did you send him to me?"

It's okay to have these feelings. Counselees can exasperate even the best of counselors. And some of their behaviors can really grate you. But at the end of the day you surrender this load to the Lord by "casting all your care upon Him, for He cares for you" (1 Pet 5: 7 NKJV). He will use this healthy Weakness to comfort you during the night and move in mysterious ways that help you the next day.

The Weakness compass point serves another purpose. Most counselor licensing agencies require a certain number of continuing education courses for license renewal. While pastoral counseling is sometimes exempt from this requirement because of the separation of church and state, the idea is a good one. It is easy to coast along once a counseling practice is established. It is easy to think we know it all and have nothing else to learn. More humble, though, is the attitude that we can always benefit from more teaching and training, knowing that the Lord will bless our lifelong efforts to deepen our capabilities as his pastoral counselors.

When it comes to the Strength compass point, most of us need some help because we don't automatically enjoy a self-image as a competent and capable counselor. We develop this image over time as a consequence of receiving positive feedback from counselees, and from seeing our professional reputation grow in our church and community.

To increase your confidence in your pastoral counseling identity, say to yourself often enough for it to really register: "I appreciate my strengths, capabilities, and developing talents as a pastoral counselor." This isn't aimed at making you cocky, but at strengthening your enjoyment of this vocation and bolstering your spirits when the occasional session falls flat, or when an encounter with a hostile or judgmental counselee takes a piece out of you. Likewise the Weakness compass point lets you say to yourself, "I am a human being with clay feet, and I am not afraid to ask for help, make an appropriate apology, or experience my need for strengthening through prayer, relationships, and community."

And when you get into the thick of a counseling session in which you have no earthly idea what to do next, just say, as Peter did when walking on water in the presence of high waves, "Help!" The Lord loves responding to his shepherds who are giving their lives to care for his sheep.

17. The Self Compass and The Congregation

You will effectively assist your congregation and lighten your pastoral counseling load by offering venues within the church for members to learn about the Self Compass, opportunities like Sunday school, book study groups, or sermons where appropriate. The larger significance of the compass model lies in the invitation it extends for understanding the self, others, and God within the church and society. This emphasis on health psychology and spirituality helps people fashion balanced personalities and make decisions that foster personal fulfillment and intimacy with God.

Each of the personality patterns described in this book exists in varying degrees of rigidity within members of the congregation. However, rigidities are made more flexible as individuals recognize and begin outgrowing the Pleaser and Storyteller, the Arguer and Rule-breaker, the Worrier and Loner, and the Boaster and Controller patterns. Not only do adults make progress removing these obstacles to Christlike personality wholeness, but they also pass on the compass template for health to their children and grandchildren.

Let's create a hypothetical scenario, in which Eva, a young married woman with two preschool children, sees you for several sessions because her husband travels in his work, and she is critical of him for not spending more time with the family. This sounds innocent enough, but you quickly discern pronounced Controller and Worrier patterns in her personality. These two opposite patterns interface within her, the avoidant Worrier pattern causing her not to trust babysitters, not to make couple's friends, and not to reach out to neighbors, but to isolate herself, leaving her terribly lonely, not simply because her husband travels, but because she is withdrawn and remote from others. Even so, Eva has never recognized this pattern in her personality because the Controller pattern drives her, not to gain insight about herself, but to find fault with her husband, no matter how hard he tries to please her.

Now if you project this rigid set of attitude-behaviors into the future of this family, you can estimate that the husband will eventually become fed up with her carping and perhaps consider divorce, while the little boys will grow up reacting daily to a perfectionist/judgmental mom, whom they will either severely rebel against by developing the antisocial Rule-breaker pattern, or comply with by forming the dependent Pleaser pattern. So by helping Eva outgrow her personality rigidities, you are helping three other people at the same time.

Eva finishes up with pastoral counseling at a fourth session, having begun to understand how the Self Compass is calling her forth to greater growth.

A month later you are pleased to learn that Eva has joined a Sunday school class where the curriculum includes one of the Compass series books. You thank God for this because you have heard on the grapevine that her husband is indeed thinking about a trial separation.

Now a year has passed since your original counseling sessions with Eva, and you've observed at a distance a gratifying development, for where Eva and her family used to look tense and hurried wherever they walked, they now appear more relaxed, taking time out to visit with other people after services or at church get-togethers. A glimpse of Eva and her husband holding hands while at the communion rail confirms your intuition that growth for this family has happened in time.

The Self Compass At Work

The Old Testament reports how the children of Israel gathered manna from heaven each day of their forty-year sojourn to the Promised Land. God had told them to gather enough of the wafer-like substance for each day's need, and they quickly found out that any form of cheating, that is, trying to hoard the manna, resulted in the manna rotting. The lesson was clear: "Trust My provision for you one day at a time and you'll be fine."

Many of the symptoms that bring people into pastoral counseling include anxiety, anger, loneliness, depression, confusion, frustration, or exasperation. In the bigger picture these symptoms are related to not trusting God one day at a time, not seeking his interactive presence in one's personality and relationships, not expanding one's behavioral repertoire to include all the creative options the Holy Spirit would like to actualize. Trying to use one or two compass points to solve all of life's problems is like hoarding manna. It leads to a rotten personality. God wants people to become flexible, creative, faith-filled persons like the Father, Son, and Holy Spirit.

Love-Stuck Parishioners

When people love others to a fault, they don't have to deal with conflict or negotiation or even the expression of individual differences. They cover up their anxiety through a public persona of loving kindness, but God knows that they are escaping the tensions of life—which require creative assertion and negotiation—by hiding from conflicts of any kind; and sure enough, their personality deteriorates into mushy sweetness, lacking the forceful depths of Christ's Self Compass. Even their children will testify in the behavioral court of life that the parent lacks assertion, perhaps by pushing behavioral boundaries that drive the parent crazy, but which the parent doesn't reign in, since they lack the firmness it takes to set and enforce appropriate boundaries.

But when teaching about the Self Compass augments pastoral counseling, people in the congregation who are stuck on the Love compass point begin to see the consequences of this rigidity, and over time make needed changes.

Assertion-Stuck Parishioners

Likewise teaching about how to disagree with one another while remaining loyal to relationships, how to express individual differences respectfully so that arguments don't escalate, and how to use diplomacy when challenging perceived unfairness, all contribute to consciousness-raising in the congregation as a whole. Church members learn to use the Assertion compass point in rhythm with the Love compass point, cutting down the incidence of divisiveness, resentment, and in-group fighting.

For example, much to your chagrin, several lay people in your church develop an ongoing argument about how the world will end and what form Christ's Second Coming will take. Because of the vehemence with which certain views are propounded, and aggressive behavior exhibited, there is danger that the cancer of dissension will invade the spirit of the church.

However, when one of the leaders in this fomenting spirit of discontent comes in for pastoral counseling, you are able to show both empathy for his belief in the rightness of his doctrine, and tolerance for his sniping at other church members, coaching him about how an overly ambitious Assertion compass point can foster resentment rather than conviviality.

By a third session the man has ventilated the original anger he came in with, and become intrigued with how in this and other instances, even clear back to grade school, he has exhibited the Arguer pattern. Because he shows some remorse now that he realizes the negative effects of his attitude on the Body of Christ, you invite him to take a growth stretch into the Love compass point by presenting his view on End Times in a special talk to the pastoral staff. This is a safe enough venue that no harm can be done, and it is an opportunity for other pastoral leaders to hear the man's theology and interact with him.

As a prelude to this meeting, you role-play with him how he can respond graciously to other points of view, and how he can present his own perspective without the dogmatic one-sidedness that presumes other views are wrong. You are coaching him on how to outgrow his paranoid suspicion, and how to experience the gratification of self-expression without hostile accusation.

The day comes, several staff members attend, the man delivers his view, then with friendliness and openness hears other possible views. You feel encouraged that his Self Compass is up and running.

Weakness-Stuck Parishioners

Quite different from Love-stuck or Assertion-stuck parishioners are those stuck on Weakness, who become nearly invisible socially. Yet how can they mature in Christ if they don't open up to relationships?

One such woman hears you preach about the Weakness compass point one Sunday and takes in the astonishing news that people like her don't have to spend their lives being shy and fearful of others, but can develop a whole Self Compass. A month later her husband catches you in a hallway and shakes your hand vigorously. "I don't know if you remember it or not, but that day you spoke about the Self Compass my wife had a great awakening. She's been a wallflower around people for years, but when we were driving up to New York for a family reunion a week later she said, 'Mike, I don't have to be like this any longer. I'm as good as the next person. I think I'm going to enjoy visiting your family.' And she did! You should have seen her telling people stories and laughing and having a great time. I want to thank you so much for setting her free."

"Praise God," you say. "I thought that was one of my less inspiring sermons so you've just made my day."

After utilizing the compass model in your pastoral ministry and pastoral counseling for some time, you realize one day that while the people are as human as ever, a change has occurred. There is an almost palpable excitement in the air, not because you changed your doctrine, which is as solid as ever, but because people themselves are changing, becoming persons who engage others in lively dialogue, warmly welcoming newcomers, and showing respect for one another's views.

Strength-Stuck Parishioners

The Strength compass point often comes to a community of believers through a time of exceptional need, and frequently takes the form of humble strength. I think God intends this congregational rhythm because confidence that arises out of strength alone is generally proud, not humble. In fact, if too much strength is taught from the pulpit and in classes, the whole church can become one big motivational seminar in possibility thinking that renders it independent of Christ, the humble servant.

I faced a crisis years ago when teaching a seminary course called "Religion and Human Behavior." The school was training students to become ministers and church leaders, but I often wondered if there wasn't too much emphasis on being strong and able.

In this course, therefore, I set out to establish with the Lord's help an open-ended learning situation, in which students could air doubts as well as faith, experience uncertainties as well as confidence, and express humanness alongside learning Christian doctrine.

Within the class setting, as a microcosm of the larger macrocosm of the church, we experienced the growth pangs of seeking to integrate the Gospel with our community of growth and learning. The first few sessions met with enthusiasm. Students shared art projects, wrote poetry, and created dramas that expressed the themes of religion and human behavior.

But during the second month this warm interpersonal atmosphere chilled. Several students who had strong Controller patterns criticized other students who were expressing vulnerability. I had not yet learned how to assertively stop this kind of self-righteous nitpicking.

After one class in particular, the icy clutches of self-consciousness gripped the whole class. People had become afraid to confide about what was really going on in their inner lives. They were falling back into a religious façade, talking about God dogmatically but not experiencing Christ existentially and interpersonally. I felt chagrined.

With a heavy heart, I paid a visit to one of the men's dorms where several students from the class resided. With five of us gathered in Carl's room, I said, "I really need help from you guys and from the Lord. I've tried to create a class where people can take the elevator down, revealing their inner hopes and struggles, their needs and dreams. But it has deteriorated into an armed camp where no one trusts anyone else." They nodded in agreement. "Can you please pray with me that Jesus might show us a way through this wilderness?"

Carl bowed his head and said, "Dear God, thank you for the opportunity you're giving us to grow and develop in this class. Forgive us for pulling back and becoming so judgmental. Please heal our wounds and set us back on the right track. In Jesus' name, Amen."

A second after he finished praying we heard a forceful knock on the door. Carl walked over and opened it. There stood a young man, barefoot and his hair soaking wet, a bath towel wrapped around his waist. He glanced around the room at our surprised faces and said, "I hope this makes some kind of sense to you, but I was just taking a shower down the hall when a voice inside me said, 'Stop. Go to Carl's room. Tell those who are gathered there that I have heard their prayer. I will show up tomorrow and set things right.'"

Leaving everyone speechless, he closed the door and returned to his shower.

I turned to the fellows in the room, whose eyes were as wide as mine. "Thanks, guys," I said, not knowing what else to say. "I'll see you in class."

The next afternoon I walked hurriedly to arrive a little early at the Religion and Human Behavior class. When I opened the door, I gasped. Instead of the normal desk placement of row upon row, someone had arranged them in concentric circles, with every desk pointing outwards, away from the center.

I panicked, wondering if this was a college prank. Should I rearrange the desks? No—a still small voice said I should simply take a seat and let the drama unfold. I did so. The first dozen students came in buzzing with talk, but as soon as they saw the odd desk configuration, they hushed and seated themselves. Finally all had found their way to a desk.

There we were, a community of persons united in Christ but divided by our lack of interpersonal maturity. Neither I nor anyone else could see anything except someone else's back.

A thunderous quiet settled over the room. Though my heart speeded up, I said nothing. What was God up to?

After a full minute of silence, one student said, "This is crazy. We're all here and we can't even see each other." Pause. A young woman said, "What has happened to our class? This feels terrible." Pause. A male voice: "Could this be a symbol of what we've been doing in here—turning our backs on each other?" I still waited. Another woman said,

"We don't have to stay this way. Let's just turn our desks around so we can talk face to face."

Desks grated against the floor as, one by one, students personally chose to again become a community.

When all the desks had turned, I stood and spoke. "This is a class in religion and human behavior. I wonder if God has shown up today to teach us something. What do you suppose it is?"

Carl cleared his throat and said, "I think that maybe the Lord has given us a speech act like he did through the Old Testament prophets and through Jesus. Maybe he's saying, 'Put away all division and strife. Open yourselves to one another, so you can all be healed.'"

With that, a man who had served on the mission field in South Africa said, "Well, now that's over with, I want to share my art project." And he did.

God's Action In Therapeutic Learning

I wonder today if God isn't saying to church communities around the world, "Turn toward one another. Bare one another's burdens so that I can make you whole. Utilize your choices for caring (Love) and courage (Assertion), humility (Weakness) and confidence (Strength)." If this is so, then we can be assured that the Trinity is at work within us, building up the Body of Christ to the glory of the Father, by the power of the Holy Spirit.

18. ADVANCED PRINCIPLES OF COMPASS THERAPY

Therapeutic techniques give you specific leverage in moving counselees through an impasse, stimulating experimentation into unused compass points, or trying out prospective solutions to longstanding or current problems.

Completing A Dream

Compass Therapy suggests that the unconscious represents the sum total of a person's life experiences stored in the vast computer-like repository of one's Mind and Heart, Body and Spirit. Unlike the Freudian perspective, which portrays the unconscious as difficult to reach and fortified with so many resistances it requires years of psychoanalysis to interpret, I believe that the unconscious is very accessible to the average person, and that God has designed the unconscious to support our holistic functioning.

Likewise, although Freud ascribed specific meanings to symbols that appeared in dreams (most commonly phallic symbols that stood for the male sex organ), I believe that dreams are more creative, and can be interpreted more intuitively, especially when they represent an unconscious search for the creative solution to an old problem never consciously resolved. So if it looks like I'll be working with a counselee for five to ten sessions, I will often say during a second session, "I'd like to invite your unconscious to participate in this counseling by giving us a meaningful dream. You might keep a notepad by your bed and record any especially vivid dream so we can talk about it."

I am working on a premise here that is rooted in compass psychotheology, the assumption that a personal and loving God sees transparently into the deepest being and motivation of every person, knowing them in a way that foresees and wishes to contribute toward their wellbeing and fulfillment. So when I invite the unconscious to manifest itself in a dream, I always pray, "Lord, bring anything to our attention that you wish."

I am not setting up the counselee to see me as a guru of interpreting dream symbols in esoteric ways, but rather setting the stage for completing the action of a dream, the part that creates anxiety or dread or anger, believing that the unconscious sometimes carries wounds not easily healed, but wants healing nevertheless.

Sarah came into a third session with such a dream. By now I had heard her story about divorcing a husband after twenty years of his relentless criticism. "Somehow I had this assumption that it was my job to make Brandon happy," she had said, "and it took all that time to figure out that he kept himself discontent to keep me on the hook."

Now in the dream she is sharing with me, she says, "I'm in this room with Brandon. There are no pictures on the walls. No decorations—just a bare room with a wooden table and two chairs. I'm sitting in one of them, feeling anxious because he's pacing back and forth, obviously thinking of some new reason why he's not happy and it's all my fault."

"How are you feeling at this point in the dream?"

"Claustrophobic and miserable, because he is my whole world and there's nothing I can do about it."

"What happens next?"

"I hear music and laughter, and when I look up I can see through a door that people in the next room are having a good time. They are enjoying each other, talking like dear friends."

"So there is life and love in the next room, but you are stuck in this bleak place that leaves your soul barren and cold. Is that right?"

"Yes. What strikes me is how dead I feel sitting there with Brandon. He never greets me or hugs me or talks to me. He just makes up things for me to do to be a 'good wife.'"

"What happens next?"

"Nothing. In the actual dream, which seemed to last forever, I just sat there like I was serving a life sentence and there was nothing I could do about it."

"And that's how the dream ended?"

"Yes. I've had similar dreams in the past, but this one really depressed me. It felt morbid. Sick. Empty."

"So it seems that your unconscious is telling us that there is no hope for you—that your life is stranded in the hell of a relationship that is killing your spirit. Yet we know from real life that you reached your limit of Brandon's top dog behavior and divorced him. How do you feel now about that divorce?"

"It was the smartest and most courageous thing I've ever done. I feel great about it. I've found a lot of meaning in the past few years."

"I wonder, then, if your unconscious simply needs an update, a way of receiving this clear message from you that you're single now and thankful for your new lease on life."

"But how can I communicate with my unconscious if it mainly remembers the twenty years of oppression I experienced with Brandon?"

"By going into the dream right now and doing whatever brings you fulfillment."

"I can do that?"

"Yes. Dreams are fluid, not set in concrete. They are creative attempts to solve life's problems, or interpret old memories in the light of new growth. You can enter an imaginary state right now and take up where the dream left off, educating your unconscious about your new life situation."

"What do I do?"

"Picture yourself sitting in this lonely room with Brandon, and all these lively people interacting with each other in the next room. What do you want to do?"

"I want to stand up, tell Brandon that he doesn't own me anymore, and walk into the other room."

"Go ahead."

"You mean I can do that?"

"It's your dream. You and God are co-architects of how your life develops. Sit at the table and then do what you feel is the next right thing."

Sarah closes her eyes. "Okay, I'm standing up now and he's glaring at me. Now he's telling me to sit back down. I'm sitting back down even though I don't want to."

"Why?"

"He's my husband and I've always done what he tells me to do."

"Yet your conscious mind knows that you're now divorced and free to choose your own way in life. Right?"

"Yes, but it's such a habit. I feel so powerless in his presence."

I stay with the coaching, knowing that sometimes counselees need encouragement to do what they need to do. "I'd like you to really concentrate on completing this dream in a way that fulfills you. What will fulfill you?"

"Standing up and walking into the other room where people are enjoying life and talking to each other. I want to join in."

"Go ahead. It's safe in this office to change the outcome of the dream."

"All right." She closes her eyes again. "I'm standing up. He's telling me to sit back down. I'm telling him that he doesn't own me anymore. That we're divorced!"

"Now complete this new action."

"I'm turning away from this dingy room and walking into the other room. Oh my goodness, several people have seen me walk in and are coming over to greet me." Her voice breaks. "They're all smiling. I feel loved."

"Let yourself engage them for about a minute."

I remain silent. Sarah's face looks serene, absorbed.

"Okay, Sarah. What are you experiencing?"

She opens her eyes. "That was a lot like how I live now. People are very open to me. I have several good friendships."

"This is a good stopping point. Let the sensations of love flow into your muscles and breathing. Your conscious has just tutored your unconscious that you are living a new and different life. What are you discovering inside yourself?"

Sarah sighs and grins. "I don't know why that seemed so hard. I guess because I spent so many years under Brandon's thumb—like being entombed in a mausoleum. But it felt great walking into the other room and interacting with everybody."

"I recommend that you take this image home with you today and go through this exercise of completing the dream several more times, experiencing the freedom and love at the end. This gives your brain time and focus to construct new RNA code that will store these memories and help extinguish the older memories of feeling trapped by Brandon. You're priming your unconscious to develop updated and more satisfying dreams about this theme in the future."

This exchange represents the deep background of counseling: shaping and sculpting a person's human nature and personality dynamics, bringing conscious and unconscious forces into rhythmic dialogue with one another. God intends the conscious and unconscious to work in complementary and harmonious ways, but this rhythm is disturbed and sometimes fixated when traumatic experiences pile up. You can never bring complete healing to a counselee, because there are too many forces in the world that work toward depersonalization of the self and fragmentation of consciousness. Yet you can make substantial strides in helping counselees adjust the particular tensions in their personality and relationships, and in so doing, they will find greater fulfillment in living.

Working with Addictions

Every church, every town, and many families know the dark effects of substance abuse that tear individuals apart. The substance might be alcohol, drugs, or food, but addiction means that a person has crossed an invisible line, before which they could exercise some cognitive discernment and volitional choice about ingesting the substance, and after which their willpower and good intentions are rendered powerless.

In my opinion, addiction groups deserve a special place in the ministry of the church, because when the spiritual fellowship of a Twelve Step program brings an addict into recovery, then pastoral counseling can focus on promoting the developmental maturity that the addictive substance formerly eclipsed.

Pastoral counselors might consider taking the initiative in contacting the central office of the granddaddy of Twelve Step groups, Alcoholics Anonymous, to see if they want to set up a meeting in the church. This puts several healing powers into motion. It signals to the community at large that this church, through an outgoing spirit of altruistic concern, provides a safe haven for people who are struggling with addiction. AA fosters a spiritual awakening by encouraging participants to humbly surrender to a Higher Power, a ministry that reaches outside of Christianity, yet because AA meetings traditionally end by saying the Lord's Prayer, assures that Christ is in their midst.

A Twelve Step group in the church strengthens the life of the community as a whole, promoting recovery from addictions that would otherwise ravage marriages, families, and neighborhoods of those living in their grip. Pastoral counseling, when it is sought, can help dismantle the rigid personality patterns that contributed to addiction in the first place, and guide the person to repair damaged relationships.

How Patterns Affect Decision-making

Compass Therapy doesn't put much stock in willpower per se, because if the will is isolated from emotion, cognition, biology, and spirituality, a person becomes more like a machine than a human being. But Compass Therapy does place considerable focus on making choices.

In the actualizing mode of making choices, individuals intuitively cross-reference their whole human nature, taking quick bearings about what the mind thinks, the heart feels, the body senses, and the spirit intuits about a possible choice. For well-integrated individuals this can occur within minutes or even seconds, helping them make decisions that remain open to feedback regarding the consequences of their choices. For instance, the apostle Paul made a tentative choice to extend his missionary journey to Asia, but the Holy Spirit gave him a dream that changed the destination to Macedonia. Paul altered his plans because his human nature was open to the influence of the Spirit (Acts 16:6-10).

However, rigid personality patterns infringe upon choice making, curtailing and distorting the process in predictable ways, depending upon where the counselee is stuck on the Self Compass. This impingement also distorts one's ability to hear from God.

Pleasers defer making choices until they are sure that other people will approve of them. Since they are one step removed from their own center of gravity, they tend to make choices that are naïve and oriented toward keeping the peace, rather than choices that reflect their true calling and potential. If possible, they try to find a stronger person who can make choices for them, so they don't feel so anxious about the decision. In this way many Pleaser-patterned persons fall prey to living out someone else's demands or expectations for them, without ever knowing that this is why they are secretly unhappy and out of touch with God's will. The pastoral counselor recognizes these features of the Pleaser pattern and works toward helping such counselees develop a more autonomous identity, learning to discern their own needs and preferences, standing up to others who are controlling them, taking the risks required for self-development, and seeking interpersonal intimacy with Christ, rather than servile placation of God.

Storytellers function in such a flurry of superficial activity and hyped-up goings-on that little or no reflective self exists, no spiritual core of contemplation where outcomes of potential choices are evaluated and selected. Rather, Storytellers are so oriented toward performing to a live audience that they thrive on the spur of the moment, making haphazard choices according to mood swings and dramatic impact on others. Here the pastoral counselor helps to activate the counselee's spiritual core. The counselor suggests that they think over what they are about to do. By modeling emotional calmness, physical relaxation, and spiritual openness, the counselor builds a bridge of communication that taps these resources within the counselee's human nature. The counselor assures them that diminishing the Storyteller pattern will not rob them of color or flair, but will help them focus more keenly on what they want to accomplish and how to do so successfully.

Arguers shrink their world into a fortified castle defended with utmost tenacity against perceived invaders, who include the rest of the world. So Arguers exclude from the decision-making process a great deal of input from other people and from God's will. Since they assume the worst in others, they guard their inner lives so tightly that even they don't know what's in their depths. Perhaps this is where pastoral counseling can offer them the most. While you can't just assure Arguers that a richer life of love, trust, and self-development lays before them, you can often develop enough of a bond that they actually begin to experience a taste of these qualities. You help them realize that too much of their decision-making is colored by negative reactions against others whom they perceive as out to get them. So when they are about to make preemptive choices during any given week, choices born in a spirit of vendetta, getting even, or spitefully cutting someone down to size, you suggest that they convert the communication into written form and read it to you. When they do so, you offer alternate ways of framing it, ways that illuminate their unconscious intentions, while anticipating the emotional reactions of the recipient. Just like Christ forms a bridge of communication between God and persons, you as a pastoral counselor form a bridge of communication between the Arguer and other people. At first it sounds like you are from another world, and in fact you are from Christ's kingdom, where paranoid blaming and arguing are not needed. In a sense you are helping the Arguer internalize not only the Gospel message of grace and forgiveness, but also the gifts of the Holy Spirit that can flow less impeded through the counselee's spiritual core, diminishing hostile decision-making in favor of wiser and more spiritually-informed choices.

Rule-breakers, too, consider others as enemies and Christ as unrealistically loving. They interrupt decision-making more from a habit of cutting red tape and gratifying impulses than from a history of spite. There is little or no cognitive inhibition to stand between their desire for something and its immediate procurement. Their impatience precludes a consideration of consequences. This mammal-like way of functioning offers a street-smart, instinctive method for sizing up people or situations in terms of getting what they want and moving on. The pastoral counselor gradually introduces the motto: Think, Think, Think. Other suggestions include taking a daily moral inventory to hear from a newly forming conscience, and making amends wherever possible to those whom they have wronged. Likewise the pastoral counselor compliments Rule-breakers every time they even approximate telling the truth, or show any sign of empathy toward someone. When they hatch a new scheme, you can compliment them on their cleverness while exploring any interpersonal impact on others. Once Rule-breakers get the hang of personality transformation, they can become very steadfast in developing a new sense of self-worth based on greater honesty with God and others, since they know the practical difference between good and evil. Thus, impulsive decision-making gradually transforms into creative problem solving, hedonistic callousness into interpersonal sensitivity.

Worriers make decisions from fear, which translates at a practical level into not choosing, not committing, not following through for fear that they might not succeed. The counselee's recollection of past history is scanty and punctuated by memories of humiliation or shame, like being teased mercilessly in physical education class for not being athletic. This kind of negative memory pattern is then projected into the future, worrying about every form that failure might take and assuming the worst possible outcome of any decision. This leads to choice-paralysis, followed by the person fading into marginal existence. The pastoral counselor needs emotional resilience to withstand all the excuses and rationalizations Worriers offer about why they can't do anything right. A counselor is tempted to try and whip the person into shape, get them on the ball, and convince them that the greatest fear is fear itself. But the real crux of therapeutic change involves joining with withdrawn counselees and reflecting back to them the bleak existence they live, even siding with them about how there is no possible way for them to choose differently. This joining does not mean giving up on them, but rather inhabiting the same space they inhabit. There is a psychodynamic law at work here that says no two beings can inhabit the same space at the same time. So, paradoxically, as you take the Worrier's "place," the Worrier makes a new choice to frame things less bleakly than you did, now standing up for their ability to choose over against your siding with a paralysis of choice. Slowly, then, they make new choices, with you expressing awe and wonder about how they are doing the very thing that's impossible to do: making their lives better. While Worriers will likely never become high achievers, the modest choices for self-development and life-improvement register over time as more contentment in life. Most significantly, the vast expenditure of energy spent on worrying becomes reallocated to creative attempts at problem solving, with more willingness to handle necessary risks.

Loners experience a general poverty of cognitive functioning, whereby left to themselves they reflect little about the quality of life, with minimal connection to people or God. But they do make decisions about narrower aspects of the world that interest them. Here they may gather a good deal of cognitive information, find stimulation, and make choices that further their interests. In working with Loners, you seek to hear and discern the one need that motivates them to see you, and through this opening you seek to pour more information about human development into their otherwise oblique thinking. They will have little patience for this, coupled with a longstanding pattern of interrupting developmental processes by walking away from the situation, so you move slowly and respectfully, accepting in advance that there may be little you can add to their life, other than a listening ear and a caring heart. Nevertheless, if you do spark a flame of interest that begins to ignite their mind, then the little opening you've created for informational enrichment and emotional comfort may expand into a relationship where they really are listening, thinking, considering, and making choices, establishing a new baseline of vital contact with the world that God has created.

Boasters can turn pastoral counseling into an extended self-referenced monologue that excludes the counselor altogether. The problem is that when it comes to making decisions, the Boaster lives in fantasyland, where dreams have already come true through the power of magical thinking, rather than through any genuine perseverance. It's not that you want to prick the bubble that carries them above ordinary people and ordinary concerns, it's that you know what they've not yet accepted: fantasy is different from reality. If you launch into coaching about taking responsibility too soon, the counselee will say, "Bye-bye." But if you express praise and admiration for the inflated accomplishments about which the counselee boasts, and then watch for holes in the argument—moments when the counselee expresses frustration, sorrow, and even resentment about why they are not getting more of their due from life—then you can reflect on a few of the probable reasons for their frustration without bursting their bubble. Over time this adds up to a relationship in which they can safely boast to their heart's content, while at the same time hearing realistic considerations regarding some of their blind spots, unrealistic expectations, and the tendency to make decisions for self-glory rather than self-development. By helping the counselee come to accept and talk openly about the way an inflated self-image short-circuits the hard work and practical steps that really do make dreams come true, you are helping the Boaster move away from the rigid pattern into a more modestly confident self-esteem that also has room for humility. Gradually they become more patient with perseverance, the needed developmental step that separates adults from children. Their decision-making becomes less pie-in-the-sky, and more informed by down-to-earth practicalities.

Controllers are filled with cognitive activity about planning, organizing, and achieving what usually amounts to laudable goals. The breakdown, however, comes from their perfectionism, an attitude that excludes the "messiness" of human emotions. Therefore, their decisions are mechanical and do not take into account real human needs. They make timelines too short, workloads too heavy, praise too rare, and pressure too constant. The pastoral counselor knows that the inner pressure driving the behavior of compulsive perfectionism does not reflect the will or character of God. The counselor also knows that while Controllers appear to be in control and on schedule at all times, the reality is they often procrastinate because they are unsure of the "perfect" decision. While orderliness is demanded by their pattern, there is always some area of their life that is falling apart, often in chaos. In other words, the curse of perfectionism is a harsh taskmaster that forces persons to make choices with a standard of expectation that no one can reasonably meet. It can liberate Controller counselees to discover through your input that human emotions are God-given means of self-awareness and interpersonal sensitivity, and that God himself is a Lover, not a perfectionist. This allows them room to breathe within overly busy schedules, surrendering to a greater degree of humanness with its accompanying needs and fair share of mistakes, as well as opportunities for warm-hearted fellowship. Gradually, their decisions become more enriched by a holistic human nature that includes responsiveness to God's unfolding will. They come to enjoy spontaneity, creativity, and serenity in ways the old Controller pattern never would have allowed.

Working With Pattern Combinations

Most counselees exhibit combinations of personality patterns, rather than a single prototype. Just as the colors of a rainbow derive from combinations of the three primary colors of red, blue, and yellow, so all behavioral manifestations derive from pattern combinations of the LAWS—Love and Assertion, and Weakness and Strength. In a first session and beyond, you can look for key expressions that give away the hidden presence of as many patterns as are incorporated into the counselee's personality. Whenever you discern too much assertion to the point of aggressive hostility, you know the counselee needs help in anger management and conflict resolution. However, the same counselee may on another occasion manifest servile dependency or histrionic melodrama, alerting you that the counselee needs help understanding and expressing healthy love.

The next counselee you see might combine an inner conflict comprised of hard-driving perfectionism on the one hand, and baffling periods of despairing helplessness on the other. As counseling proceeds you facilitate a more introspective rhythm between Strength and Weakness, eventually helping your counselee outgrow the radical swings between omnipotence and impotence, replacing these with modulated rhythms of Strength and Weakness as normative for the human condition, yet uniquely expressed by the counselee.

Sometimes you are struck by how different patterns of personality emerge in different interpersonal environments. For instance, a woman uses her whole Self Compass at work, where she is known for her diplomatic assertion, healthy confidence, caring for others, and enough humility to admit when she is wrong or needs help. At home, however, her personality collapses. Due to an abusive relationship with her father that she never successfully challenged, she has married a narcissistic and argumentative man who has reduced her to a withered hulk of nerves. He's just asked his most recent girlfriend to move in with them and instructed the wife to be nice to her. Somehow you want to focus on each of the compass points, drawing upon her successful expression of them at work, and helping her learn how to use them in her chaotic home life. In this case, each session suggests one or another compass point that through its lack of use contributes to her misery, but through its embryonic expression in sessions adds momentum to her actualizing growth. Eventually she learns how to extract herself from the abusive relationship by using her whole Self Compass in both her personal and professional life.

In some sessions you'll not refer to the Human Nature Compass or the Self Compass at all, but they are still guiding you to see transparently into your counselee's being, inspiring you to create growth experiments and well-timed interpretations, all designed to move the counselee forward toward actualizing wholeness.

Creating Forward Movement

Compass Therapy suggests that most sessions are characterized by empathic listening, the reflecting of counselee feelings, and the offering of cognitive insights about the situation at hand. Yet beyond this basic rhythm of listening and interpreting, Compass Therapy actively engages counselees using their whole human nature, the dynamic Self Compass, and a willingness to encourage humor, surprise, and lively interaction, all of which contribute to interesting, even intriguing, pastoral counseling.

This doesn't mean that you put a whole lot of energy into each session, for that would wear you out. Instead, you sit back in a comfortable chair and listen to your counselee, letting your own unconscious, with its resourcefulness in remembering personality theory, counseling theory, Scripture, and communication principles, guide you in ways that allows the counseling process to breathe with life. *You trust the process of gradual growth and development.* Even flat or seemingly dead-end sessions can contribute to overall progress, which entails valleys as well as peaks.

If counseling gets stalled at a particular impasse, then you can shift your vantage point, focusing on a different compass point or dimension of human nature that resonates with the counselee's energy. To further enrich your counseling repertoire with twenty-five therapeutic techniques that promote counselee transformation, I suggest you read *Christian Counseling That Really Works* (2006). And if you are interested in advanced techniques for facilitating intervention in cases involving personality disorders, I recommend *Compass Therapy: Christian Psychology In Action* (2008).

While bringing your human presence and active trust in the Trinity to each session, once the session is over, you let it all go, knowing that worry doesn't move things forward. Thoughtful, intuitive action during sessions, coupled with the therapeutic value of people speaking their inner truth as best they understand it, does move them in the direction of compass health and wholeness. You can count on it!

19. THE TRINITY AND PASTORAL COUNSELING

For centuries, Christianity didn't know quite what to do with the Trinity, other than mention the Trinity during congregational recitation of orthodox creeds or at baptism.

But in light of what we have learned in the study of interpersonal psychology, we can now grasp that the Trinity is actually the ontological foundation of human personhood and interpersonal relationships. The Father, Son, and Holy Spirit are three Persons in one God who actualize their love through mutual indwelling, and who invite human beings to share in this Trinitarian intimacy.

Compass Therapy is constructed on a Trinitarian platform that supports the interconnections between personhood, personality, and interpersonal relationships.

Thus, the compass approach to pastoral counseling invites the Trinity's participation in the counseling process. This can take the form of prayers for counselee blessing, trust in divine guidance during sessions, and response to the Father's desire to fashion persons into the image of Christ by the power of the Holy Spirit. Wisdom from the Word of God commingles with empirical research from behavioral science to create a unified field theory of psychospiritual growth and fulfillment. The counselee, then, experiences an integration that encompasses reason and faith, the natural and supernatural.

Compass Therapy suggests that the Trinity expresses an abiding presence in pastoral counseling, healing and transforming personality and relationships in Christlike directions, for the wellbeing of persons and the glory of God.

Now in drawing this book to a close, I want to thank you for sharing in this collegial conversation. Please receive my appreciation for all the good work you do and the many people you help.

Here is my prayer for us both:

"Dear heavenly Father, thank you for our calling to the field of pastoral care and counseling. Empower us with the Holy Spirit that we might contribute hope and healing to people in both church and community. Help us wisely blend Scripture and science in ways that accomplish your purposes. Thank you for loving, helping, and abiding with the counselees we serve. In Jesus' name, Amen."

APPENDIX:
PERSONALITY PATTERNS IN A NUTSHELL

While the *Diagnostic and Statistical Manual of Mental Disorders (DSM)* term "personality disorder" captures the severity and rigidity of an inflexible personality pattern, it can have a side effect of diminishing self-esteem, creating a sense of futility about the future (Corrigan, 1998; Holmes & River, 1998). Research shows that counselees often internalize stigmatizing labels and believe they are less valued because of their disorder (Link, 1987; Link & Phelan, 2001; Corrigan & Miller, 2004). Further, self-stigmatizing can lead to decreased participation in counseling.

On the other hand, interventions that challenge self-stigmas and facilitate empowerment are more likely to increase counselee engagement in all aspects of care (Speer et al., 2001). For this reason the Compass Therapy approach to pastoral counseling emphasizes the big picture of a *health psychology* that encompasses a counselee's personality rigidity, providing positive directions for growth even while presenting counselees with relevant aspects of their trends or patterns.

The eight personality patterns presented in Part III include: dependent Pleaser, histrionic Storyteller, paranoid Arguer, antisocial Rule-breaker, avoidant Worrier, schizoid Loner, narcissistic Boaster, and compulsive Controller.

These counselee-friendly labels contain both a clinical element from *DSM*, which reflects a worldwide consensus

about their reality, and a common sense element that counselees can understand and remember. Referring to the patterns as rigid attitude/behaviors that the counselee is
outgrowing creates a spirit of warranted optimism. You
might say, "I really like how you turned a deaf ear to the
inner voice of your old compulsive Controller pattern in
order to enjoy that party so much." Or, "It sounds like the
dependent Storyteller pattern is making a bid to create false
guilt again." Or, "I can see why you stole so many CDs from
your employer; the Rule-breaker pattern makes it seem
totally to your advantage to do so."

Clinical observations demonstrate the therapeutic benefit
of increased self-knowledge generated by this type of skillful
interpretation of counselee behavior (Levy, 1990; Meissner,
1991). Here, then, are the personality patterns in a nutshell.

Dependent Pleaser Pattern: Love Compass Point

The dependent pattern is widely recognized in clinical
literature. Both Freud's and Abraham's concept of an "oral
character" views the pattern as exhibiting many traits of in-
fancy: total dependency, lack of assertion, a tendency to
cling to others, separation anxiety, and insatiable needs for
constant care, affection, and support (Freud, 1938; Abraham, 1911/1968). Fenichel (1945) aptly describes the oral
dependent as a "love addict."

Horney (1945) describes the "compliant type" as a person
who chronically "moves toward people" with pleasing and
placating behaviors. Fromm (1947) sees the dependent pattern as creating a "receptive orientation" characterized by
interpersonal naiveté and Pollyannaish gullibility. Tyrer
agrees that there is a Pollyanna-like view of the world in
which they regard duplicitous motives of manipulative individuals with imperceptive childlike trust (Tyrer, Morgan,
Cicchetti, 2004).

As in all personality patterns, the actualizing quality of a
compass point is lost when taken to an extreme and left un-

balanced by the opposite compass point. Therefore, even though dependent counselees want to give and receive love more than anything else in the world, genuine love—which requires the integration of Strength and Assertion with Love and Weakness—eludes them. The overblown Love compass point skews behavior toward self-sacrifice without self-preservation, submissiveness without assertion, and giving without receiving. Beneath their warmth and niceness lies a desperate search for acceptance and approval (Pincus & Wilson, 2001).

Rejection is feared more than aloneness, so the dependent takes no risks toward individuality or independent thought or action that might lead to alienation from sources of nurturance (Beck et al., 2007).

Unconscious forces are set in motion by these dynamics. A dependent-patterned person can be seen as cooperative and gracious by others, yet has actually undergone identity foreclosure, meaning that self-development is arrested with a childlike focus on safety and gratification, much like a fetus needs the mother to feed it and provide oxygen through the umbilical cord. Not knowing they can cut the psychological umbilical cord by developing the healthy expressions of Strength and Assertion, they fear independence instead of acquiring it. Nor do they comprehend that healthy people would find them more lovable for replacing clinging vine dependency with authentic selfhood.

The over-exaggeration of the Love compass point alone strands a counselee in a sea of masochism. It's not that dependent Pleasers like pain, because they don't. It's just that they don't realize how this subservient pattern creates the fundamental reason for this distress: the pain of feeling constantly on edge about keeping people happy and the pain of needing other's approval for whatever they do (Cogswell & Alloy, 2006).

The dependent Pleaser pattern exists as a pure prototype of fixation on the Love compass point, but can occur in combination with the adjacent compass points of either Strength or Weakness. When combined with the Strength compass point, counselees develop compulsive controlling features; combined with the Weakness compass point, the dependent develops avoidant depressive features. In all cases, however, the Assertion compass point is decommissioned.

Histrionic Storyteller Pattern: Love Compass Point

The first psychosocial descriptions of what is now known as the histrionic personality disorder came from nineteenth century German psychiatry and described the symptoms of emotional impulsiveness (Feuchtersleben, 1847), underlying irritability, and the need to refer every life occurrence back to one's self (Griesinger, 1867).

The "hysterical personality" was erroneously presumed to be a condition found only among women. There has since emerged abundant clinical evidence to support the existence of Casanovas and bons vivants.

Early psychology gave various labels to the histrionic pattern like the "choleric character" (Heymans & Wiersma, 1867), the "fickle temper" (McDougall, 1932), and the "extroverted-intuitive type" (Jung, 1921).

The perspective that most accurately foresaw today's clinical consensus cites "a preference for theatrical pathos...to dream themselves into big purposes in life, the playing with suicide, the contrast between enthusiastic self-sacrificial abandonment and a naive, sulky, childish egotism, and especially a mixture of the droll and tragic in their way of living" (Kretschmer, 1926, p. 141).

For histrionics, love is everything. To be the best of friends, to find a new romance, to pluck down the moon and the stars. Unlike the Pleaser pattern, which is self-effacing and non-competitive, the histrionic pattern distorts the Love compass point into an extroverted demand for reassurance that one is attractive and loveable (Millon & Davis, 1996).

Compass theory labels this the histrionic "Storyteller" pattern to highlight the distinctive feature of constant talking. So great is the need for center stage that the Storyteller butts into conversations, hijack topics, makes eye-catching gestures, displays erratic moods, hurries or slows the cadence of speech for dramatic effect, and weaves fragments of storylines into a patchwork of disjointed tales (Montgomery, 2008). The hearer wants to say, "Please get to the point," or "Now how does this relate to what we were talking about?" but finds this difficult because the histrionic actually engages in an extended monologue.

This stream-of-consciousness talking is often punctuated by overreacting to something that someone says which the Storyteller takes personally. These ideas-of-reference comprise beliefs that other people's statements or acts have special reference to oneself when in fact they do not. They make prototypal Storytellers prone to disrupt normal communication with bursts of envy, flirtatious innuendos, rolling of the eyes, crocodile tears, and hilarity. Especially if they feel insulted, they resort to pouting and moping. For milder histrionics, similar manipulative ploys are acted out at a lesser level of intensity, all with the aim of capturing and keeping interpersonal attention.

Histrionics invest their prime energy in the Love compass point, with little awareness of diplomatic assertion from the Assertion compass point, a stable sense of self-worth from the Strength compass point, or humility from the Weakness compass point. In fact, they avoid the Weakness compass point by reflexively exiling unpleasant thoughts or feelings to the unconscious. Without Weakness, however, histrionic Storytellers do not accept their losses nor develop a teachable spirit. Impulsive behaviors supplant introspection or constructive reflection and undercut learning from life experiences.

The histrionic Storyteller pattern exists as a pure prototype of fixation on the Love compass point, yet can incorporate features drawn from the adjacent compass points of Strength or Weakness. In the case of Strength, the counselee develops narcissistic self-glorification; in the case of Weakness, the Storyteller develops avoidant self-recrimination with depressive features. If there are marked swings between the Love and Assertion compass points, then cyclothymic or bipolar features prevail. More typically, though, the opposite polarity of Assertion is shut down and prohibited expression.

Paranoid Arguer Pattern: Assertion Compass Point

Paranoia is a term characteristic of the Arguer pattern meaning "to think beside oneself." The term "paranoia" is of Greek origin, found in medical literature over 2000 years ago, and precedes the writings of Hippocrates, capturing the sense of a delusional belief system that emphasizes suspicion and hostility. Unwilling to follow the lead of others, and accustomed to trusting only themselves, the paranoid Arguer pattern carries out a reconstruction of reality in accordance with its dictates.

Freud (1938) describes paranoia as a "neuropsychosis of defense," capturing how the pattern wards off reality through the defense mechanisms of denial and projection. Shapiro (1965) adds that the projection of unacceptable feelings and impulses onto others both eliminates guilt and accounts for the lack of intrapsychic conflict.

Unwilling to acknowledge their faults or weaknesses, Arguers shore up their self-esteem by projecting personal shortcomings onto others, believing that it is others who are malicious and vindictive. This pattern is expressed in a variety of forms. They include: the "combative type" who wants to fight the world, the "eccentric type" who withdraws yet harbors persecutory delusions, or the "fanatic type" who recruits others into secret sects (Schneider, 1950).

Horney (1950) observes that paranoid-patterned persons exhibit "sadistic trends" that distract them from their hid-

208

den inferiority. By blaming and attacking others they build a counterfeit self-esteem. This obnoxious behavior acts to isolate them from meaningful or intimate relationships, further confirming their suspicion that the world is against them, and that "the blame for their failure (lies) solely on external hindrances" (Kraepelin, 1921, pp. 268-271).

Compass theory has selected the term "Arguer" to stand for the perpetual contrariness and automatic argumentation that dominates the paranoid's perceptual field. There are endless ruminations or "subliminal arguments" about past injustices or wounds to their pride; current quarrelsomeness with family members, work associates, or even strangers; and plans-in-preparation for arguing their case in the immediate future. Like a disputatious defense attorney, they are always on the job, considering no detail too trivial for possible use in winning a battle in the courtroom of daily life (Montgomery, 2008).

Fearing the vulnerability that accompanies love, Arguers harden their hearts to the needs or suffering of others, ruling out the possibility of intimate bonding (McHoskey, 2001). Instead, the Love compass point is used to manufacture displays of false charm. So too, the humility and soul-searching of the Weakness compass point are twisted into self-pity, where Arguers berate people, institutions, or life itself as unfair to them. The Strength compass point inflates the Arguer with airs of self-importance and invincibility, even illusions of omnipotence (Noonan, 1999), and a burning need to get their way (Reid, 2005).

These compass distortions mean that paranoid Arguers believe people are out to get them, and that they are justified in the hostility they direct towards others (Coolidge, 2004). They levy castigating remarks with impunity since they feel no remorse. Antagonism and suspecting the worst in others color all that they do (Sheldon & Stevens, 1943).

The paranoid pattern exists as a pure prototype of fixation on the Assertion compass point with an aggressive trend. It is also found in combination with the adjacent compass points of either Strength or Weakness. In the case of Strength, paranoid aggression combines with narcissistic pomposity or compulsive criticalness; with Weakness, the paranoid Arguer develops avoidant depression or schizoid detachment. In all instances, the opposite polarity of Love is decommisioned and prohibited expression.

Antisocial Rule-breaker: Assertion Compass Point

The pattern of behavior that *DSM* nomenclature presently defines as the antisocial personality disorder was described in nineteenth century clinical literature as "moral insanity," in which "the moral or active principles of the mind are strangely perverted or depraved" (Pritchard, 1835, p. 85). The original perception concerning the term "psychopathic personality" later came to include a broader definition that encompassed such traits as guiltlessness, incapacity for love, impulsivity, failure to learn, untruthfulness, and superficial charm (Cleckley, 1964). Others described the antisocial pattern as the "manipulative personality" (Bursten, 1972), the "impulse ridden character" (Reich, 1976), and "pure interpersonal hostility" (Kiesler, 1996).

More recently, the term "sociopathic" has replaced "psychopathic" to reflect the social rather than the purely psychological origins of the pattern. In agreement with Millon, I view the current *DSM* designation of the "antisocial personality disorder" as overemphasizing delinquent and criminal behaviors (Millon & Grossman, 2007b). A number of contemporary studies focus on the organizing principle of nonconformity rather than criminality as the defining trait of the antisocial pattern (Vasey et al., 2005; Vien & Beech, 2006).

Compass theory employs the term "Rule-breaker" as a significant feature of the antisocial mindset, because it reflects a willful stand to live outside the boundaries of custom and the rule of law, and because counselees readily understand the term.

On the positive side, most children and adolescents normally experiment with breaking rules as part of their coming of age, discovering their personal power over-and-against the socializing forces of a tribe, family, religion, or schooling. Carl Jung (1989) experienced this phenomenon as a child, when he carved a little manikin and hid it under an attic slat where no one could find or harm it. He later wrote that the ability to possess and keep this secret helped provide him with a personal identity.

A healthy dose of antisocial sentiment fosters the willingness to take risks, test boundaries, think outside the box, and not take someone else's "no" as the last word on a possible goal or action (Montgomery & Montgomery, 2006). Einstein's biographer explains that Einstein so hated formal schooling that he devised a scheme by which he received a medical excuse from school on the grounds of a potential nervous breakdown. He convinced a mathematics teacher to certify that he was capable to begin college studies without a high school diploma (Frank, 2002).

However, these positives reach the point of diminishing returns when an aggressive trend constricts into a rigid template. Now the antisocial Rule-breaker pattern overtakes the personality. Callous adventurism eclipses compassion or sensitivity to others (Raine et al., 2004).

Suspicion and hostility are common to both the Rule-breaker and Arguer patterns, the clear indication of an exaggerated Assertion compass point. But Rule-breakers are more opportunistic, impulsive, and shamelessly exploitive than Arguers. Nor do Rule-breakers cultivate secretive persecutory delusions, since they are quite open about touting "the law of the jungle" as the wisest philosophy of life.

While paranoid histories can include humiliating failures that reveal the discrepancy between their glorified self-image and lack of personal development, antisocial Rule-breakers are notably resourceful. They learn from life experience that little will be achieved without substantial effort and cunning, and that desired goals must be accomplished by one's actions (Kotler & McMahon, 2005).

If Rule-breakers overly use the upper quadrants of the Self Compass, what happens to the lower quadrants? The Love compass point is warped into a façade of charm that masks the hidden intent to exploit. The Rule-breaker represses feelings of tenderness, for this would give others the advantage. The avoidance of healthy Weakness keeps them from empathizing with other's pain or admitting any faults. It is precisely this lack of empathy combined with entitlement that creates a "superego lacunae"—a massive deficiency in social conscience (Kernberg, 1995). Thus a Rule-breaker is well equipped to exploit people's weaknesses or trust.

The antisocial Rule-breaker pattern sometimes combines with the narcissistic, histrionic, or schizoid patterns, which serve the antisocial agenda by adding features of grandiosity (distorted Strength), extroverted charm (distorted Love), or lone wolf cunning (distorted Weakness). Antisocial Rule-breakers employ their creativity to assimilate characteristics drawn from other patterns in order to better manipulate others while camouflaging their true intent. The healthy dimension of the Love compass point is avoided at all costs.

Avoidant Worrier Pattern: Weakness Compass Point

Avoidant Worriers retreat from human interaction even though they are often creative and emotionally sensitive. Their hypersensitivity is demonstrated by "affects (that) are so powerful...they must avoid everything which might arouse their emotions," notes Bleuler. "The apathy toward the outer world is then a secondary one springing from a hypertrophied sensitivity" (1950, p. 65).

Philosopher Sören Kierkegaard recorded in his journal that he viewed himself as "melancholy, soul-sick, profoundly and absolutely a failure in many ways" (Dru, 1959). This sorrowful existence is captured in Emil Kretschmer's (1925) description of the hyperaesthetic type: "There is a constant self-analysis and comparison: 'How do I impress people? Who is doing me an injury? How shall I get through?' This is particularly true of gifted, artistic natures...They are (people)...whose life is composed of a chain of tragedies, a single thorny path of sorrow."

Karl Menninger (1930) describes the avoidant Worrier as an "isolated personality" prone to failure in interpersonal situations—as "wistful 'outsiders' who long to dive into the swim of things and either don't know how or are held back by restraining fears."

While Worriers may be talented in solitary endeavors, the interpersonal anxiety that plagues them causes an overload of core fear. Kurt Schneider (1950) calls the avoidant pattern the "aesthenic personality," citing "a deeply rooted insecurity and the lack of any robust self-confidence. This personality type is continually ridden with a bad conscience and are the first to blame themselves for anything that goes wrong. They are people forever dissatisfied with themselves through life."

Portrayals such as these affirm the present day perspective that a biological predisposition to generalized anxiety and depression can exist within the avoidant Worrier pattern. Characteristics of the avoidant Worrier are frequently cited in the literature on depression (Skodal et al., 2005).

The exaggeration of Weakness, accompanied by an abandonment of the Strength compass point, locks the Worrier-patterned person into a lifestyle of helplessness and incompetence. Worriers see themselves as inadequate and boring, lacking enough skill or intelligence to succeed. Although the longing for intimacy remains strong, they do not build successful relationships because their fear of rejection and ridicule overwhelms them. They hold back from friendships and avoid social encounters to guard against the risk of disappointment. Nor do they stand up for themselves, preferring to retreat instead.

For the Worrier counselee, potential energy from the Strength compass point collapses into the sinkhole of a failure mentality. Even though the avoidant Worrier's personality pattern sabotages growth and development, it appears to Worriers as if other people's frustration with them is confirming their fundamental assumption: "People don't like me. I can't do anything right." This self-blame for their lack of social connection intensifies the self-alienation that reinforces their isolation from others (Huprich, 2005).

The avoidant pattern exists as a pure prototype of fixation on the Weakness compass point in a withdrawn trend, but in some cases bonds with an adjacent compass point of either Love or Assertion. In the case of Love, the Worrier develops dependent submission to another person. In the case of Assertion, the Worrier develops paranoid prickliness or antisocial hostility. In every instance, however, the opposite polarity of Strength is shut down and prohibited from expression.

Schizoid Loner Pattern: Weakness Compass Point

In early clinical literature, this pattern was referred to as the "shut-in" personality to describe behavior that defended against anxiety by "shutting out the outside world, a deterioration of interests in the environment, a living in a world apart" (Hoch, 1910). The term, "autistic personality" highlights schizoid Loner tendencies to "narrow or reduce their external interests and contacts" and develop a "preoccupation with inward ruminations" (Kraepelin, 1919).

Eugene Bleuler coined the word "schizoid" and observed that such individuals were "incapable of discussion" (1924, p. 441.) Carl Jung developed his concept of "introversion" in part to describe the social detachment of Loner-patterned persons, remarking that "they have no desire to affect others, to impress, influence, or change them in any way, which may actually turn into a disregard for the comfort and well-being of others" (1921, p. 247).

The current view holds that the schizoid-patterned life is a solitary one characterized by dissociation of the mind from the body, heart, and spirit. The result is emotional deadness and social apathy (Montgomery & Montgomery, 2007).

While the schizoid Loner and avoidant Worrier patterns are both trapped on the Weakness compass point, they distance themselves from people for two different reasons. Worriers are shy and sensitive, yearning for intimacy yet held back by fears of ridicule and rejection; whereas Loners withdraw because of "an indifference to everything—to friends and relations, to vocational enjoyment, to duties or rights, to good fortune or bad" (Bleuler, 1950, p. 40). The rewards and pleasures of human companionship mean nothing to them.

Karen Horney notes that schizoids actively "move away from people" by forming an impenetrable shell that makes others fade out of consciousness (1945/1994). Not only do others disappear off their radar screen (West et al., 1995), but their own emotions evaporate as well (Haznedar et al., 2004). This life plan has its merits in that schizoid Loners maintain simple lives, untroubled by feelings, impervious to relationships, and undisturbed by inner conflicts. In fact, if a person wants to live an ascetic life that is celibate and single, the schizoid pattern offers the structure and function for doing so. Perhaps this accounts for the secret superiority often noted in schizoid counselees (McWilliams, 1994). Compass theory posits that this tendency reflects the psychodynamics of a tightly repressed Strength compass point that acts out in the form of unconscious narcissism (Montgomery & Montgomery, 2006). Millon notes: "Fantasy in a schizoid-like person can betray the presence of a secret grandiose self that longs for respect and recognition and offsets fears that the person is really an outcast" (2004, p. 390).

While everyone needs a rhythm that includes occasional withdrawal and detachment, the schizoid Loner's selection of isolation as a long-term coping pattern leads into dangerous territory: a solitary confinement that begins as a retiring lifestyle, but can spiral into schizotypal eccentricity, possibly leading to several types of schizophrenia (Collins et al., 2005; Giesbrecht, 2007). This detachment reflects the interpersonal truth that human beings need social stimulation. When they isolate from the rewards and consensual validation that society normally provides, their psyche can succumb to excessive daydreaming, voices that speak from illusory entities, and the formation of an alternate psychic reality. The psychospiritual energy for actualizing growth, when not pursued, doesn't just disappear; unconscious forces convert it into the landscape of the Loner's version of the universe.

In Self Compass terms, the Loner-patterned person lacks esteem for self or others (Strength compass point), love for self or others (Love compass point), and courage to take risks for self-development or the bettering of circumstances (Assertion compass point). The energy from these compass points is shunted into exaggerated weakness, creating a depersonalized existence.

Narcissistic Boaster Pattern: Strength Compass Point

Narcissism is a well-founded concept in clinical literature. Freud describes the "narcissistic libidinal type," focusing on how easily this individual assumes social leadership: "The main interest is focused on self-preservation; the type is independent and not easily overawed...They readily assume the role of leader, give a fresh stimulus to cultural development or break down existing conditions" (1931/1950, p. 249).

Horney employs an effective metaphor in conveying the essence of narcissism as "self-inflation," which, "like economic inflation, means presenting greater values than really exist" (1939, pp. 89-90). The "phallic-narcissistic character" captures the essence of this pattern for Reich, whose colorful description conveys his view: "If their vanity is offended, they react with cold disdain, marked ill-humor, or downright aggression. Their narcissism is expressed not in an infantile but in a blatantly self-confident way, with a flagrant display of superiority and dignity" (1949, p. 217-218).

For Leary (1957), the narcissistic pattern shows self-confidence based on "adjustment through competition" that seeks superiority and fears inferiority. Kiesler employs concrete adjectives to create a vivid picture of the narcissistic pattern as brazen, cocky, boastful, pushy, egotistical, self-enthralled, and unable to ask for help with anything (1996).

Recent research supports the prevalence of the narcissistic personality pattern in the general population and its association with considerable prevalence among men, whose rates exceed those of women (Stinson et al., 2008).

Compass Therapy employs the term "Boaster" to describe the narcissistic pattern because whether verbally or through body language, Boasters constantly display their achievements and strive to appear as better looking, more confident, wealthier, more brilliant, more accomplished, and more important than others (Witte et al., 2002). However, their self-glorification reflects more illusion than fact, since narcissists usually lack the motivation, discipline, and skills required to ground these attributes in reality (Aizawa, 2002).

Narcissists puff up their self-image to avoid activating fears of inferiority (Beck et al., 2007). They frequently wound family, friends, and work associates by placing themselves on a pedestal from which they pass judgment on perceived imperfections in others, secretly seeking to safeguard their aura of positive superiority by putting other people down (Gosling et al., 1998).

The Boaster pattern shares with the Storyteller pattern a need for admiration. But while Storytellers actively solicit attention from others, Boasters disdain this dependency, feeling that it would limit their power. Instead, the Boaster employs a coolly superior style to elicit other's admiration.

The Strength compass point is exaggerated with the need to be right about everything, which they share with compulsive Controllers. But their entitlement, a defining trait of this pattern, lifts them above the rules of convention and engenders haughtiness (Montgomery, 2008).

A paradox worth noting is that while Boasters show remarkable indifference to the needs, feelings, and wellbeing of others, they nevertheless feel very vulnerable to criticism or being ignored, together with a strong desire for loving support and admiring deference from others (Benjamin, 2003). This leads to unbalanced relationships in which the narcissistic Boaster remains emotionally immature and incapable of sustaining the rhythmic reciprocity required for intimacy. It is common for narcissists to experience several divorces over the course of their lives (Beck et al., 2007).

Compulsive Controller Pattern: Strength Compass Point

Freud describes the compulsive personality pattern as the "anal character" which is manifested in people who are "exceptionally orderly, parsimonious, and obstinate" (1925).

In an expansion of this concept, Abraham describes the "obsessional type" as experiencing "pleasure in indexing and classifying...in drawing upon programs and regulating work by timesheets...The forepleasure they get in working out a plan is stronger than their gratification in its execution." And regarding a judgmental attitude toward others, he writes: "They are inclined to be exaggerated in their criticism of others, and this easily degenerates into carping" (1927, pp. 148-152). Reich (1949) emphasizes the presence of emotional repression and rigid body armor in "the compulsive character." He notes that compulsives are reserved and self-possessed, hiding their emotions from themselves and others. Shapiro (1965) observes the rigidity of the Strength compass point with its self-conscious control in "obsessive-compulsive" types: "These people not only concentrate; they always seem to be concentrating." The underlying motiva-

218

tion that drives this pattern is control of oneself and external circumstances, a control that is achieved by assuming an "omniscience and omnipotence (that) can give one a false illusion of certainty" (Salzman, 1985, p. 19).

An explanation of the near synonymous terms "obsessive" and "compulsive" may prove helpful. In the nineteenth century, Von Krafft-Ebing (1868) introduced the German word for compulsive, "Zwang," to refer to patients with compulsively constricted thinking. A year later Griesinger (1869) used the word compulsive or "Zwang" to describe patients who incessantly cross-examined themselves about what to do and how to do it. By the early twentieth century this German word had found its way into American translations as "compulsion" and British translations as "obsession" (Millon et al, 2004).

Today, obsessive-compulsive symptoms refer to specific repetitive thoughts and acts that are beyond volitional control; e.g., washing one's hands frequently. When applied to a personality style, the obsessive-compulsive personality disorder is essentially the same as the compulsive disorder.

To simplify this duplication of terms, Compass Therapy defines the compulsive Controller personality pattern as a rigid style of functioning in which a counselee is obsessed with perfection and compelled to emphasize control above all else. They must appear to others as strong and decisive in every situation. The key word here is "appear," because the overblown Strength is founded upon a reaction formation against ever-present anxiety (Weakness).

Though it masquerades as socially sanctioned and virtuous behavior, the compulsive Controller pattern more accurately functions as a micromanager that sizes up any situation or person as falling short of an inner ideal of perfection. Even a pastoral counselor is in for trouble when suggesting that compulsives might enjoy life more if they surrender this grim rule-keeping existence. What we have here is a paradox: the very personality pattern that promises society the most stable, responsible, and consistent behavior actually poisons self and others through critical judging and emotional formality.

The Strength compass point forms the underlying girder for the compulsive Controller pattern, with secondary support from the Assertion compass point when opposition occurs. This makes compulsive control a top dog pattern, since it favors controlling others over being controlled by them. The Weakness compass point is denied and converted into doubly energizing its opposite compass point of Strength.

The Love compass point is stripped of heartfelt feelings and turned into doing one's duty. The nurturance, patience, and forgiveness that love requires are displaced by criticalness, impatience, and grudge bearing. Controllers busy themselves attending to what they consider of utmost importance: striving, achieving, and staying organized (Shostrom & Montgomery, 1978).

Though the compulsive pattern exists as a pure prototype that is fixated on the Strength compass point, it can combine with the adjacent compass points of Assertion or Love. In the case of Assertion, the Controller displays the argumentativeness of the paranoid pattern, except the focus lies with legalistic points about the "rightness" of their judgment. In the case of binding with the Love compass point, the compulsive displays conscientious "goodism," striving to be perfectly good at rescuing everybody. In all of these instances, the opposite polarity of Weakness is avoided at all costs, save for the fact that it haunts the unconscious with anxiety.

In summary, whereas personality patterns fixate life into rigid molds of self-defeating behavior, Compass Therapy seeks with God's help to facilitate healthy growth toward personality wholeness and relational fulfillment.

BIBLIOGRAPHY

Abraham, K. (1968). Notes on the psychoanalytic investigation and treatment of manic-depressive insanity and allied conditions. In *Selected papers of Karl Abraham*. London: Hogarth. (Original work published 1911).

Adams, J. (1986). *Competent to counsel*. Grand Rapids, MI: Zondervan.

Adler, A. (1994). *Understanding human nature*. Rockport, MA: One World. (Original work published in 1927).

Aizawa, N. (2002). Grandiose traits and hypersensitivity of the narcissistic personality. *Japanese Journal of Educational Psychology, 50,* 215-224.

Allport, G. W. (1937). *Personality: A psychological interpretation*. New York: Holt, Rinehart, & Winston.

Anandarajah, G. (2008). The 3 H and BMSEST models for spirituality in multicultural whole-person medicine. *Journal of American Family Medicine, 6,* 448-458.

Andrews, J. D. (1991). *The act of self in psychotherapy: an integration of therapeutic styles*. New York: Gardner.

Assagioli, R. (2000). *Psychosynthesis*. MA: Synthesis Center.

Augsburger, D. W. (1995). *Pastoral care across cultures*. Louisville, KY: Westminster John Knox Press.

Beck, A., Freeman, A., & Davis, D. D. (2007). *Cognitive therapy of personality disorders* (2nd ed.). New York: Guilford.

Benjamin, L. S. (1996). *Interpersonal diagnosis and treatment of personality disorders*. New York: Guilford.

————. (2003). *Interpersonal diagnosis and treatment of personality disorders* (2nd ed.). New York: Guilford.

Benner, D. (2003). *Strategic pastoral counseling: A short-term structured approach*. Grand Rapids, MI: Baker.

Berkouwer, G. C. (1962). *Man: The image of God*. Grand Rapids, MI: Eerdmans.

————. (1954). *The nature of Christ*. Grand Rapids, MI: Eerdmans.

Berne, E. (1985). *Games people play*. New York: Ballantine.

Blair, R. J. R. (2005). Applying a cognitive neuroscience perspective to the disorder of psychopathy. *Journal of Development and Psychopathology, 17*, 865-891.

Bleuler, E. (1950). *Dementia praecox*. New York: International Universities Press.

Bloesch, D. G. (2002). *The church*. Downer's Grove, IL: InterVarsity Press.

————. (1995). *God the Almighty*. Downer's Grove, IL: InterVarsity Press.

————. (2000). *Holy Scripture: Revelation, interpretation and inspiration*. Downers Grove, IL: InterVarsity Press.

————. (1997). *Jesus Christ*. Downers Grove, IL: InterVarsity Press.

Boisen, A. T. (1936). *The exploration of the inner world*. New York: Harper & Brothers.

Brammer, L., Shostrom, E. L., & Abrego, P. (1993). *Therapeutic psychology*. Englewood Cliffs, NJ: Prentice-Hall.

Buber, M. (1970). *I and thou*. New York: Charles Scribner.

Bursten, B. (1972). The manipulative personality. *Archives of General Psychiatry, 26*, 318-321.

Cleckley, H. (1964). *The mask of sanity* (2nd ed.). St. Louis, MO: Mosby.

Clinebell, H. (1984). *Basic types of pastoral care and counseling: Resources for the ministry of healing and growth*. Nashville, TN: Abingdon Press.

Cogswell, A., & Alloy, L. B. (2006). Neediness and Axis II pathology. *Journal of Personality Disorders, 20,* 16-21.

Collins, G. (2007). *Christian counseling: A comprehensive guide.* Nashville, TN: Thomas Nelson.

Collins, L. M., Blanchard J. J., & Biondo, K. M. (2005). Behavioral signs of schizotypy in social anhedonics. *Journal of Schizophrenia Research, 78,* 309-322.

Coolidge, E. L., DenBoer, J. W., & Segal, D. L. (2004). Personality and neuropsychological correlates of bullying. *Personality and Individual Differences, 36,* 1559-1569.

Cooper-White, P. (2006). *Many voices: Pastoral psychotherapy in relational and theological perspective.* Minneapolis, MN: Fortress Press.

Corrigan, P. W. (1998). The impact of stigma on severe mental illness. *Cognitive and Behavioral Practice, 5,* 201-222.

Corrigan, P. W., & Miller, D. (2004). *Shame, blame, and contamination: A review of the impact of mental illness stigma on family members.* Manuscript submitted for publication.

Corsini, R., Ed. (2001). *Handbook on innovative therapy* (2nd ed.): *Ch. 1, Actualizing therapy.* New York: Wiley.

Corey, G. (2009). *The art of integrative counseling.* Boston: Brooks Cole.

Crossley, J. P., & Salter, D. P. (2005). A question of finding harmony: A grounded theory study of clinical psychologists' experience of addressing spiritual beliefs in therapy. *Journal of Psychology and Psychotherapy: Theory, Research, and Practice, 78,* 295-313.

Cunningham, D. S. (1997). *These three are one: The practice of Trinitarian theology.* Hoboken, NJ: Blackwell.

Davies, J. C. (1991). Maslow and theory of political development. *Political Psychology, 12,* 289-420.

Dittes, J. E. (1999). *Pastoral counseling: The basics.* Louisville, KY: Westminster John Knox Press.

Dru, A. (Ed.) (1959). *The journals of Kierkegaard.* New York: Harper & Row.

Ellis, A., & Harper, R. (1997). *A new guide to rational living.* Englewood Cliffs, NJ: Prentice Hall.

Erikson, E. H. (1993). *Childhood and society.* New York: Norton. (Original work published in 1950).

———. (1959). *Identity and the life cycle.* New York: International Universities Press.

Erickson, M. J. (1998). *Christian theology (2nd ed.).* Grand Rapids, MI: Baker Books.

Farris, J. R. (2002). *International perspectives on pastoral counseling.* Philadelphia: Haworth Press.

Fenichel, O. (1945). *The psychoanalytic theory of neurosis.* New York: Norton.

Frankl, V. (1972). *The doctor and the soul.* New York: Knopf.

———. (1984). *Man's search for meaning.* New York: Simon & Schuster.

Freud, S. (1989). *An outline of psycho-analysis.* New York: Norton.

———. (1938). *The basic writings of Sigmund Freud.* New York: Modern Library.

———. (1933). *The interpretation of dreams.* NY: Norton.

Fromm, E. (1947). *Man for himself.* Greenwich, CT: Fawcett.

Gerkin, C. V. (1984). *Living human document.* Nashville, TN: Abingdon.

Giesbrecht, T., Merckelbach, H., Kater, M., & Sluis, A. F. (2007). Why dissociation and schizotypy overlap: the joint influence of fantasy proneness, cognitive failures, and childhood trauma. *Journal of Nervous and Mental Disease, 195,* 812-818.

Gosling, S. D., John, O. P., Craik, K. H., & Robins, R. W. (1998). Do people know how they behave? Self-reported act frequencies compared with online codings by observers. *Journal of Personality and Social Psychology, 74,* 1337-1349.

Greencavage, L. M. (1990). What are the commonalities among the therapeutic factors. *Professional Psychology, 21,* 372-378.

Grenz, S. J. (2001). *Rediscovering the triune God: The Trinity in contemporary theology.* Minneapolis: Augsburg.

———. (2001). *Social God and the relational self.* Louisville, KY: Westminster John Knox Press.

Hans, S. L., et al. (2004). Offspring of parents with schizophrenia: Mental disorders during childhood and adolescence. *Schizophrenia Bulletin, 30,* 303-315.

Haznedar, M. M., Buchsbaum, M. S., Hazlett, E. A., Shihabuddin, L., New, A., & Siever, L. J. (2004). Cingulate gyrus volume and metabolism in the schizophrenia spectrum. *Schizophrenia Research, 71,* 249-262.

Heymans, G., & Wiersma, E. (1909). Beitrage zur speziellen psychologie auf grundeiner massen-untersuchung. *Zeitsehrift Fuer Psychologie, 42, 46, 49, 51.* In T. Millon & R. Davis. (1996). *Disorders of personality, DSM IV and beyond.* New York: Wiley.

Hiltner, S. (1949). *Pastoral counseling.* Nashville, TN: Abingdon.

Hoch, A. (1910). Constitutional factors in the dementia praecox. *Review of Neurology and Psychiatry, 8*: 463-475.

Holmes, E. P., & River, L. P. (1998). Individual strategies for coping with the stigma of severe mental illness. *Cognitive and Behavioral Practice, 5,* 231-239.

Horney, K. (1945). *Our inner conflicts.* New York: Norton.

———. (1950). *Neurosis and human growth.* New York: Norton.

Hunter, R. J., & Ramsay, N. (2005). *New dictionary of pastoral care and counseling.* Nashville, TN: Abingdon Press.

Huprich, S. K. (2005). Differentiating avoidant and depressive personality disorders. *Journal of Personality Disorders, 19.* 659-673.

James, W. (1950). *The principles of psychology.* New York: Dover. (Original work published in 1890).

———. (2007). *Varieties of religious experience: A study in human nature.* Charleston, SC: BiblioBazaar. (Original work published in 1902).

Johnson, P. E. (1953). *Psychology of pastoral care.* Nashville, TN: Abingdon.

Jung, C. G. (1968). *Man and his symbols.* New York: Dell Publishing.

———. (1933). *Modern man in search of a soul.* New York: Harcourt Brace.

———. (1996). *Psychology and religion.* New Haven, CT: Yale University Press.

———. (1958). *The undiscovered self.* NY: Little Brown.

Kernberg, O. (1995). *Aggression in personality disorders and perversions.* New Haven, CT: Yale University Press.

Kiesler, D. J. (1996). *Contemporary interpersonal theory and research: Personality, psychopathology, and psychotherapy.* New York: Wiley.

Koenig, H. G. (2004). Religion, spirituality and medicine: Research findings and implications for clinical practice. *Southern Medical Journal, 97,* 1194-1200.

Kollar, C. (1997). *Solution-focused pastoral counseling.* Grand Rapids, MI: Zondervan.

Kotler, J. S., & McMahon, R. J. (2005). Child psychopathy: Theories, measurement, and relations with the development and persistence of conflict problems. *Clinical Child and Family Psychology Review, 8,* 291-325.

Kraepelin, E. (1921). *Manic-depressive insanity and paranoia.* Edinburgh: Livingstone.

Kretschmer, E. (1926). *Hysteria.* New York: Nervous and Mental Disease Publishers.

Kusher, M. G., & Sher, K. J. (1991). The relation of treatment fearfulness and psychological service utilization. *Professional Psychology, 22,* 196-203.

LaCugna, C. (1991). *God for us: The Trinity and Christian life.* San Francisco: Harper Collins.

Ladd, G. E. (1993). *A theology of the New Testament.* Grand Rapids, MI: Eerdmans.

Lazarus, A. (2006). *Brief but comprehensive therapy: The multimodel way.* New York: Springer.

Leary, T. (1957). *Interpersonal diagnosis of personality: A functional theory and methodology for personality evaluation.* New York: The Ronald Press.

Levy, S. T. (1996). *Principles of interpretation: Mastering clear and concise interventions in psychotherapy.* Northvale, NJ: Jason Aronson.

Link, B. G. (1987). Understanding labeling effects in the area of mental disorders: An assessment of the effects of expectations of rejection. *American Sociological Review, 52,* 96-112.

Link, B. G., & Phelan, J. C. (2001). Conceptualizing stigma. *Annual Review of Sociology, 27,* 363-385.

Lowen, A. (1975). *Bioenergetics.* New York: Coward, McCann & Geoghegan.

MacArthur, J. (2005). *Counseling: how to counsel biblically.* Nashville, TN: Thomas Nelson.

Malony, H. N., & Augsburger, D. (2007). *Christian counseling: An introduction.* Nashville, TN: Abingdon.

Martens, W. H. J. (2005). Multidimensional model of trauma and correlated antisocial personality disorder. *Journal of Loss and Trauma, 10,* 115-129.

Maslow, A. H. (1971). *The further reaches of human nature.* New York: Viking.

———. (1998). *Toward a psychology of being (3rd ed.).* New York: John Wiley. (Original work published in 1962).

May, R. (1989). *Art of counseling.* New York: Gardner Press. (Original work published in 1965).

———. *Love and will.* New York: Norton. (Original work published in 1969).

McDougall, W. (1932). *Introduction to social psychology.* New York: Scribners.

McHoskey, J. W. (2001). Machiavellianism and personality dysfunction. *Personality and Individual Differences, 31,* 791-798.

McWilliams, N. (1994). *Psychoanalytic diagnosis.* New York: Guilford Press.

Meissner, W. W. (1991). *What is effective in psychoanalytic therapy: The move from interpretation to relation.* Northvale, NJ: Jason Aronson.

Menninger, K. (1930). *The human mind.* New York: Knopf.

Miller, W. R., & Thoreson, C. E. (2003). Spirituality, religion, and health: An emerging research field. *American Psychologist, 58,* 24-35.

Millon, T., & Davis, R. (1996). *Disorders of personality: DSM-IV and beyond.* New York: Wiley.

————. (2000). *Personality* disorders *in modern life.* New York: Wiley.

Millon, T., & Grossman, S. (2007a). *Moderating severe personality disorders.* New York: Wiley.

Millon, T., & Grossman, S. (2007b). *Overcoming resistant personality disorders.* New York: Wiley.

Millon, T., Millon, C., Meagher, S., Grossman, S., & Ramnath, R. (2004). *Personality disorders in modern life.* New York: Wiley.

Moltmann, J., Ed. (1997). *How I have changed: Reflections on thirty years of theology.* Harrisburg, PA: Trinity Press, 11.

————. (1993). *The Trinity & the kingdom.* Minneapolis, MN: Fortress Press.

Montgomery, D. (1996). *Beauty in the stone: How God sculpts you into the image of Christ.* Nashville: Nelson.

————. (2006). *Christian counseling that really works: Compass therapy in action.* Morrisville, NC: Lulu Press.

————. (2008). *Compass therapy: Christian psychology in action.* Morrisville, NC: Lulu Press.

————. (2007). *Faith beyond church walls: Finding freedom in Christ.* Morrisville, NC: Lulu Press.

Montgomery, D. & Montgomery, K. (2009). *Christian personality theory: A self compass for humanity.* Morrisville, NC: Lulu Press.

————. (2006). *Compass psychotheology: Where psychology & theology really meet.* Morrisville, NC: Lulu Press.

————. (2007). *The self compass: Charting your personality in Christ.* Morrisville, NC: Lulu Press.

————. (2009). *Trusting in the Trinity: Compass psychotheology applied.* Morrisville, NC: Lulu Press.

Moss, D. (2002). The circle of the soul: The role of spirituality in health care. *Journal of Applied Psychophysiology and Biofeedback, 27,* 283-297.

Noonan, J. R. (1999). Competency to stand trial and the paranoid spectrum. *American Journal of Forensic Psychology, 17,* 5-27.

Nouwen, H. (1979). *The wounded healer.* New York: Doubleday/Image.

Oates, W. (1982). *Pastoral counseling.* Louisville, KY: Westminster John Knox Press.

Oden, T. C. (1984). *Care of souls in the classic tradition.* Minneapolis, MN: Fortress Press.

Orlinsky, D. E., Grawe, K., & Parks, B. K. (1994). Process and outcome in psychotherapy. In A. E. Bergin & S. L. Garfield (Eds.). Handbook of psychotherapy and behavior change (4th ed.). New York: Wiley.

Patton, J. (1985). *Is human forgiveness possible?* Nashville, TN: Abingdon.

Perls, F. (1989). *Gestalt therapy verbatim.* Gouldsboro, ME: Gestalt Journal Press.

Pincus, A. L. (1994). The interpersonal circumplex and the interpersonal theory: Personality and its pathology. In S. Strack & M. Lorr (Eds.), *Differentiating normal and abnormal personality* (pp. 114-136). New York: Springer.

Pincus, A. L., & Wilson, K. R. (2001). Interpersonal variability in dependent personality. *Journal of Personality, 69,* 223-251.

Plutchik, R., & Conte, H. R. (1997). *Circumplex models of personality and emotions.* Washington, D.C.: American Psychological Association.

Pritchard, J. C. (1835). *A treatise on insanity.* London: Sherwood, Gilbert and Piper.

Raine, A., Ishikawa, S. S., Arce, E., Lencz, T., Knuth, K. H., Bihrle, S., et al. (2004). Hippocampal structural asymmetry in unsuccessful psychopaths. *Journal of Biological Psychiatry, 55,* 185-191.

Reich, W. (1980). *Character analysis.* New York: Farrar, Straus and Giroux. (Original work published in 1933).

Reid, W. H. (2005). Delusional disorder and the law. *Journal of Psychiatric Practice, 11,* 126-130.

Rogers, C. (1965). *Client-centered therapy: Its current practice, implications, and theory.* Boston: Houghton-Mifflin.

———. (1961). *On becoming a person.* Boston: Houghton Mifflin.

Salekin, R. T., Leistico, A. R., Trobst, K. K., Schrum, C. L., & Lochman, J. E. (2005). Adolescent psychopathy and personality theory: The interpersonal circumplex: Expanding evidence of a nomological net. *Journal of Abnormal Child Psychology, 33,* 445-460.

Satir, V. (1983). *Conjoint family therapy.* Palo Alto, CA: Science and Behavior Books.

Schneider, K. (1950). *Psychopathic personalities* (9th ed.). London: Cassell. (Original work published in 1923).

Seeman, T. E., Dubin, L. F., & Seeman, M. (2003). Religiousity/spirituality and health: A critical review of the evidence for biological pathways. *American Psychologist, 58,* 53-63.

Shapiro, D. (1965). *Neurotic styles.* New York: Basic Books.

Shaw, A., Joseph, S., & Linley, P. A. (2005). Religion, spirituality, and posttraumatic growth: A systematic review. *Journal of Mental Health, Religion, and Culture, 8,* 1-11.

Shay, J. J. (1996). Psychotherapy with the reluctant male. *Psychotherapy, 33,* 503-513.

Sheldon, W. H., & Stevens, S. S. (1942). *The varieties of temperament: A psychology of constitutional differences.* New York: Harper.

Shostrom, E. L. (1976). *Actualizing therapy: Foundations for a scientific ethic.* San Diego: Edits.

Shostrom, E. L., & Montgomery, D. (1978). *Healing love: How God works within the personality.* Nashville, TN: Abingdon.

———. (1986). *God in your personality.* Nashville, TN: Abingdon.

———. (1990). *The manipulators.* Nashville, TN: Abingdon.

Skodol, A. E., Grilo, C. M., Pagano, M. E., Bender, D. S., Gunderson, J. G., Shea, M. T., et al. (2005). Effects of personality disorders on functioning and wellbeing in major depressive disorder. *Journal of Psychiatric Practice, 11,* 363-368.

Speer, P. W., Jackson, C. B., & Peterson, N. (2001). The relationship between social cohesion and empowerment: Support and new implications for theory. *Health Education and Behavior, 28,* 716-732.

Stajkovic, A. D. (2006). Development of a core confidence-higher order construct. *Journal of Applied Psychology, 91,* 1208-1224.

Steketee, G., & Frost, R. (2003). Compulsive hoarding: Current status of the research. *Clinical Psychology Review, 23,* 905-927.

Stinson, F. S., Dawson, D. A., Goldstein, R. B., Chou, S. P., Huang, B., Smith, S. M., Ruan, W.J., Pulay, A. J., Saha, T. D., Pickering, R. P., & Grant, F., (2008). Prevalence, correlates, disability, and comorbidity of DSM-IV narcissistic personality disorder: Results from the wave 2 national epidemiologic survey on alcohol and related conditions. *Journal of Clinical Psychiatry, 69,*1033-45.

Stone, H. (2001). *Brief pastoral counseling.* Minneapolis, MN: Augsburg Fortress.

Sullivan, H. S. (1953). *The interpersonal theory of psychiatry.* New York: Norton.

Tracey, T. J. G. (2005). Interpersonal rigidity & complementarity. *Journal of Research in Personality, 39,* 592-614.

Trueblood, D. E. (1957). *Philosophy of religion.* New York: Harper & Row.

Tyrer, P., Morgan, J., & Cicchetti, D. (2004). The Dependent Personality Questionnaire (DPQ): A screening instrument for dependent personality. *International Journal of Social Psychiatry, 50,* 10-17.

Vasey, M. W., Kotov, R., Frick, P. J., & Loney, B. R. (2005). The latent structure of psychopathy in youth; A taxometric investigation. *Journal of Abnormal Child Psychology, 33,* 411-429.

Vaughan, R. (1994). *Pastoral counseling and personality disorders.* Lanham, MD: Sheed & Ward.

Vien, A., & Beech, A. R. (2006). Psychopathy: Theory, measurement, and treatment. *Trauma, Violence, and Abuse, 7,* 155-174.

Wampold, B. E. (2001). *The great psychotherapy debate: Models, methods and findings.* Mahwah, NJ: Lawrence Erlbaum.

West, M., Rose, M. S., & Sheldon-Keller, A. (1995). Interpersonal disorder in schizoid and avoidant personality disorders: An attachment perspective. *Canadian Journal of Psychiatry, 40,* 411.

Wicks, R. W., Ed., Parsons, R. D., Ed., & Capps, D., Ed. (2003). *Clinical handbook of pastoral counseling, vol. 3.* Mahwah, NJ: Paulist Press.

Wise, C. A. (1951). *Pastoral counseling: Theory and practice.* New York: Harper.

Witte, T. H., Callahan, K. L., & Perez-Lopez, M. (2002). Narcissism and anger: an exploration of underlying correlates. *Psychological Reports, 90,* 871-875.

INDEX

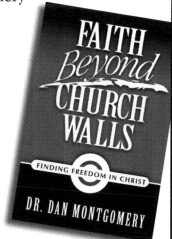

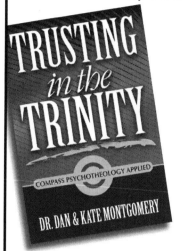

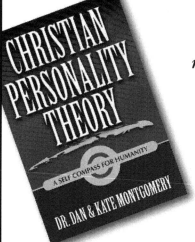
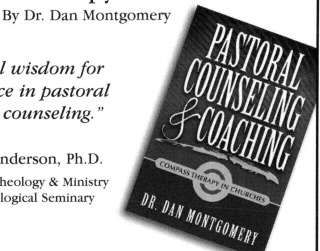

8460408R0

Made in the USA
Lexington, KY
03 February 2011